Light HouseKeeping

A Journal depicting our Family's life
on Three Penobscot Bay Lighthouses
and
My husband's life at an isolated, three-man Lighthouse
South of Vinalhaven Island, Maine.

By

Pauline E. "Fitzgerald" DeRaps

To Mark
Linda & Mark
Something to read
when your bored ♡
Love,
Pauline E. Fitzgerald De Raps

Published and copyrighted by
FogHorn Publishing, Inc.
P.O. Box 68, Wells, Maine 04090
207-646-7000
www.FogHornPublishing.com

Designed by FogHorn Publishing, Inc.

Printed in the United States of America
First Printing 2006

FogHorn Publishing is a proud supporter of the lighthouse preservation
efforts of the American Lighthouse Foundation

P.O. Box 889, Wells, Maine 04090
207-646-0245
www.LighthouseFoundation.org

The Diary of Life

In the book of life you are writing
  You alone are the one
Who can write upon these pages
  A true record of what you have done.

The day the last page is finished,
  It is certain you cannot know,
So think wisely of what you are writing;
  Try and make it worthwhile as you go.

When the diary of life has been written
  And is finally yellow with age;
When all the deeds of your lifetime
  Have been entered upon each page;

Will the acts that before you are listed
  Be things that you are proud to review
As there on the desk of eternity
  The diary shall open anew?

by — Virginia Katherine Oliver

My Side of the Story:
Light HouseKeeping
By
Pauline E. "Fitzgerald" DeRaps

A Woman's View of LightHouse Keeping!

Ernie joined the United States Coast Guard, 18th October, 1955. For the next nine months, life cruised right along for us. He did his duty at the Base in Rockland, Maine; coming home every other night and every other weekend. I stayed at our duplex apartment, across the driveway from my parent's home, and took care of our year old son, Tommy Joe.

One night in late July 1956, after dinner and our son was tucked into bed, Ernie said he wanted to talk to me about something. "How would you like to live in a lighthouse?" he asked. "There's a need for an Officer in Charge, at Monhegan Island Light Station, and I thought it might be an interesting tour of duty plus the family would be together."

Being together sounded very good to me, also, Ernie would be able to see Tommy growing and watch his cute antics. But, what would our duties be? Where was Monhegan? How long would we be there? Questions, questions. Ernie hardly knew how to answer them, because he had never lived at a lighthouse, except for two or three days at Mark Island Light Station as a Relief Keeper.

I scurried around for a map, and, found that Monhegan was a small island out in the Atlantic Ocean, about ten miles off the coast of Maine. That didn't sound like any big deal. I used to go by ferry to the island of Islesboro to visit my grandparents, and that trip was fun.

"Yes" I said. "Let's do it. It will be something different. We can write our memoirs about living in a lighthouse and any experiences we have. I will miss being near my parents, but we do what we have to do."

I kept thinking this will be a cinch. Just put our goods on a big ferry, sit back, and enjoy a calm, pleasurable ride from the wharf in Port Clyde, pass the Georges Islands and onto tiny Monhegan. How wrong can anyone be!

Prior to moving day, we cleaned out our duplex apartment. All furnishings, except our son's crib, his toys, and my sewing machine, were put in storage, as the lighthouse was completely furnished. Only our personal belongings and food, would go with us.

Our last night on the mainland, was spent with my folks, talking, drinking tea, and wondering what the morrow would bring.

All too soon, 8 A.M. came, and, a small Coast Guard truck backed up to the porch, and our things were placed aboard. Farewell hugs and kisses passed around to the family, and we were off in our old '48 Hudson Commodore.

First stop was the Coast Guard Base in Rockland to pick up government supplies and Ernie's duty station transfer papers.

We stopped at a restaurant for lunch. On our way again, motoring south on State Route 131 from Thomaston to Port Clyde, the fresh smell of the coastal waters filled the air. At Port Clyde, we bought more food, mostly perishables, to supplement the staples brought from home. We had heard there was a small store on the island, but didn't know what they carried, only knew the prices would be higher than on the mainland.

Finally, we were at the wharf, and everything was toted again. Personal gear, food, government supplies, etc.

While waiting for Ernie to park the car, I sat on an old fish box, holding Tommy. I was approached by a young "Coastie" who asked if I was Mrs. DeRaps. Nodding an affirmative, he informed me that the ferry for Monhegan had already left, and there would not be another until the next day at 10 A.M. Frustrated, I didn't know if to laugh or cry. Good thing I was sitting, when informed of our dilemma.

Then my hubby arrived. One look at my face told him something was wrong. We had a major problem. It was solved, too quickly, to suit me.

I had not noticed a Coast Guard boat tied up to the pier, I had my eyes on the horizon, and lobster boats. The reason the Coastie and boat were there, was us.

"Oh no, fellows," I said, "You're kidding. You don't mean to tell me you're taking us to our island home in that little boat?"

I had been on the open sea only once before, on a deep sea fishing trip. And, I swore by all that was holy, I would NEVER be out there again in a small boat. I was so nauseated on that fishing trip, it took me days to get over the effects.

All the time I'm talking, our provisions were being loaded aboard the craft. When I saw the fellows cover everything with a large canvas, then lash it down, my knees started to shake. I was told a breeze was making up, that we might run into a swell or two, my teeth started to chatter. All ready, I felt ill and we hadn't even left the dock. Better get myself under control, for my son's sake, if nothing else.

Our little fellow, of twenty one months, was taking everything in stride. He loved boats and getting a ride in one was Paradise. That tiny rascal had the time of his life. For his mother, it was a different story.

As the crew carefully assisted me aboard, the boat swayed and pitched just enough to knock me off balance. Helping hands reached out just in time to prevent a serious fall.

After getting my balance, they passed Tommy to me. I took him inside the small cabin, laid him on a bunk and strapped him down. The long car ride and exciting daily events had tired him out, so he was ready for a nap, I hoped. I stayed with him until he fell asleep. I preferred to stand outside and hang on, rather than stay under cover in the cabin and smell the horrible diesel fumes.

Actually, the first three miles were quite pleasant. I was surprised. The small islands East of Muscongus Bay gave us shelter from the southwest winds and helped keep the inshore waters fairly smooth. Soon, we approached the Georges Islands. One of them was the duty station (Burnt Island Lifeboat Station) of our crew and base for the forty foot utility craft we were being transported on.

After passing Burnt Island, we were in the wide open Atlantic Ocean. The last seven miles to Monhegan Island, were to be a living hell for me.

I enjoy reading sea stories, and have heard many a wild tale, but, never had I seen such a change in a sea. Almost instantly, we started to toss and turn, to pitch and yaw. A short time ago, the sea had slight ripples and was colored a sapphire blue. Now, the sea was a black, ugly, ferocious monster. The wind screamed and howled. The boat felt out of control. Huge waves battered us. One monstrous wave brought green water cascading over us. I got soaked to the skin.

Somehow, my husband got me inside the cabin, and on the small bunk beside our sleeping son. Neither of us knew how Ernie did it, as I was so scared, my fingers had to be pried from the safety strap I was holding and my feet were practically glued to the deck.

Being inside the cabin, away from the sight of that horrible sea, didn't stop me from being afraid. I was petrified. I was positive I would never see land again, or our families. Our lives were hanging in the balance.

It made me furious to hear the crew referring to the weather as just a little blow. Little blow! Hell, it was a hurricane, as far as I was concerned. Of course, I didn't stop to think, they were used to being out in weather worse than this.

To me, there is nothing worse than the stench of diesel fuel. Down in the cabin, the air reeked of it. No girls room here, and I was gagging. I found a bucket and used it - was tossed to the deck and used the bucket again. A few nauseous sessions left me so weak I could hardly hold up my head, let alone the bucket. Sitting on the cabin deck, was easier than trying to stay on the bunk. Getting tossed around on the floor was better than falling on it.

Oh God, how much longer? How much more can I endure? I'm so tired! I'm exhausted, completely washed out, though not OFF the boat, thank God. Not yet anyway!

Just when I'm at my lowest ebb, my husband poked his head inside the cabin door and asked me to come topside. With his help, I dragged myself up and out. I inhaled salt air. I gulped and swallowed salt water and spray. The freshness gave me some strength. The helmsman told me to look dead ahead. I made out a long, gray something that looked like the top of a whale's back. "It's Monhegan Island," he shouted above the half-gale wind and engine noises.

That statement, plus the fact the terrible seas were subsiding, gave me added strength.

By 4 P.M., I was getting my first real view of the island. It gave me the impression of a stalwart place.

I was in the cabin taking care of our son, when we arrived at Monhegan's wharf and moored. You just can't imagine my astonishment when coming up on deck. Have you ever seen what it looks like beneath a wharf?? Well, that's exactly what I saw. We had arrived at dead low tide, with just enough water under us to bring the boat beside the pier. The deck of the wharf was twenty feet above my head.

Beautiful terra firma was up there, but how in the dickens was I supposed to get to it? A dirty, slimy, greasy ladder bolted to the side of the pier, stayed there, just waiting for me to climb it. I was wearing a long, soaking wet, cumbersome coat and I was still weak from the tumultuous trip. But, the desire to reach solid ground pushed me forward and up.

Cautiously, I stepped to the boat's gunwale and to the first rung. So far, so good! Putting my bare hands on that clammy, mucky, slippery ladder, was something else. I don't mind getting my hands dirty, but, I had to grab hold of an area that few people did, due to the extreme low tide.

MONHEGAN
A WHALE OF A PLACE

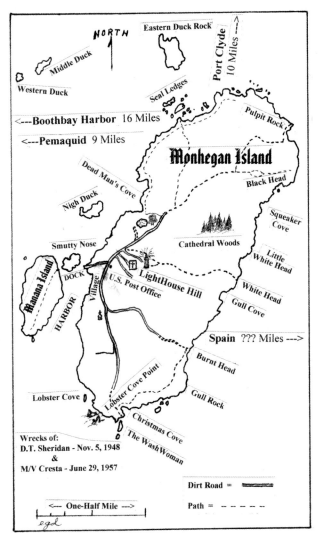

Needless to say, I finally accomplished those twenty feet. At the top, helping hands grasped me, while I struggled to straddle over the last ladder rung.

I was jubilant and full of thanks, when my feet touched solid ground. I wanted to bend down and kiss that sweet earth, but, too many people were watching. It's a wonder I didn't do it anyway, I was so relieved the trip was over.

Looking around me, I thought, "Good Grief" the whole island's population must have turned out to witness the arrival of their new lighthouse keeper and his family. The miserable specimen of humanity I made, must have given them something to talk about for weeks. My wind-blown, wet, matted hair; my face chalk white. My hands and the front of my coat completely covered with dirt, oil and slime. I didn't see any cameras, thank GOD.

At the dock was an old, battered, grayish blue, Dodge pickup truck - the Coast Guard limousine. Ernie took pity on me and asked the Relief Keeper to take me up to the lighthouse. Ernie and the crew, with help from some Monheganites, labored hauling our supplies up to the dock from the 'forty footer' boat. You talk about exhausting work. Everyone earned their supper that night.

Monhegan Lighthouse

Of course, I didn't have the foggiest idea where I was being taken, except that I knew it was to the Lighthouse, somewhere up there on Lighthouse Hill. Within a very short distance from the dock, the old Dodge power wagon was grinding its gears as we weaved over and around big rocks in the road. Road? More like a winding path up a mountain side. Tommy thought the slipping and sliding was positively thrilling. From the dock to the Lighthouse was, no doubt, little over a half mile. By the time we reached the house, I thought I had climbed Mt. Everest, at least.

We were helped down from the truck and left to fend for ourselves, while the driver returned to the dock to help load and bring up our goods. That is, if there was anything left to bring by the time they reached the top of the dock. The milk will have turned to cottage cheese, I'm sure. ...

From our viewpoint atop Lighthouse Hill, Tommy and I could survey most of the island. We could see where the dock was, but not much of the goings on. Houses were in the way. I stood there, taking in my new surroundings and decided I am going to like this place. I looked down, patted my tummy, and thought; "How about you, little one? How did you like your first, wild, boat ride?" I haven't stated that I was four months pregnant.

MONHEGAN'S WHITE HEAD ACROSS GULL COVE

Grasping Tommy by his hand, I said, "Let's go take a look inside our new home. We'll wait for Daddy for our tour around the grounds."

While Tommy ran from room to room, I checked the kitchen, seeing that's where I spend a good deal of my time. Very adequate with plenty of cupboard space. A pantry. Heavens, I haven't seen one of these in years. I started opening doors, and all I saw was shelves and shelves full of first aid equipment and materials. I thought, 'What in the world was all that stuff doing there'? I didn't know at the time, but soon found that, there in our pantry were medical supplies for the whole island.

Off each corner of the kitchen was a tiny room, with the exception of the larger pantry. One space held the washing machine, one was an outside entry, another was Ernie's (the Officer in Charges') office. Neat arrangement. Through the pantry or a small hall you could enter the dining room, living room and a nice side porch — all glassed in. Bedrooms and a bath were upstairs.

Hey!! Why don't the lights work?? I thought it strange, so went around checking everything electrical. Nothing worked. I tried the stove. Ahhh, gas. Now if I can find out how to work it - a cup of hot coffee would be nectar from the gods, just about now.

ANGEL WINGS AT MONHEGAN

We didn't have much of a rest, before we heard the power wagon grinding up the hill. A sound we would get used to shortly. By the time the truck was unloaded, it was time for the relief keeper to show Ernie how to light the light. While that was going on; I spent my time making beds, putting clothes away, making a spot for Tommy's toys (one of those tiny spots off the kitchen corners would be perfect - the one where the washing machine stood),taking care of the food and wondering what to have for a night meal. Our tummies were so tired, it must be something light, a good hot bowl of soup sounded wonderful. Maybe a "sandbidge," Tommy called them. Rest a bit in our living room, then, blessed sleep. No one would have to rock us.

Next morning, a half hour after sunrise, the light in the tower was extinguished and the lens was covered with its cloth skirt. At 8 o'clock the Stars and Stripes were raised to the top of the flagpole and saluted. Then, as with all our days, the workday began. After the light was heated and lit, one half hour before sunset, and the flag was lowered at sunset, the nights were ours.

While Ernie was attending to his duties, Tommy and I got dressed and began breakfast. After his cereal, Tommy wanted a piece of toast. I plugged in the toaster, and again, nothing happened. We decided to wait for Daddy and see if his expertise in electricity could help us.

"My Dear, didn't I tell you, no one on Monhegan has regular electricity, everyone must have their own generator and batteries," Ernie informed me with a grin. "Come here," he said, "and I'll show you how it works." With that Ernie took us outside and in one of the many out buildings, the one nearest to the kitchen, he opened its door and there sat this monster of a machine — a generator to make electricity. No way was I going to attempt to start it, so Ernie was a sweetheart and did it for me. What a racket. Worse than a train going by next to your bedroom window. It was terrible.

I got an idea!!! If we wanted a slice of toast, butter the bread and put it in the fry pan, over the gas stove. Ah, ha! Don't need the generator for that. Let's see how many ways I can make do. I thought about winter coming on, and needing lights early, just have to go to bed earlier. Anyway, like everything else, we got used to the noise. After a while, neither did it bother us to have 150,000 candle power of light shining out overhead and into the hall ways.

The dwelling was built in 1824 and rebuilt in 1850. Nice Maine granite foundation. Down cellar, where I went only one time, were huge cisterns to hold our water supply, (I was happy anytime it rained) and a coal furnace. All of that was for Ernie to take care of. I cleaned the two story house, and sometimes I swept the loooong enclosed walkway, just to the bottom of the tower stairs, leading up to the light. Outside, besides the generator building, were smaller buildings. One used for paint storage, another stored fuel for the generator and kerosene for the oil burning light in the tower. There was also an un-roofed enclosure where coal was stored for the furnace. Way down back was a building used for garage work.

Thinking about the truck, I might add, there were only two roads, such as they were, on the island. One from the dock to the lighthouse and the other from the dock to the store and just a smidgen more. I think it stopped by the church. Everyone walked paths from house to house. The schoolhouse was off the road up Lighthouse Hill. The nine children who attended, walked to and from.

Summertime, the population ballooned to hundreds. By fall, dropped to about 68 people. The greatest pastime was walking out back of the lighthouse to an area known as Cathedral Woods, to see the flora and fauna. If you kept on walking you came to the cliffs called Black Head. You could look down about 160 feet to see the Atlantic crashing against the rocks. And, wouldn't you know, that area produced our first patient.

It seemed like we had hardly found our way from the kitchen to the upstairs bath, I know we had been on the island a very short time, when we heard hollering. Someone came running for our help. Ernie grabbed the ever ready first aid kit and took off on the run. A young lady had advanced too close to the edge of a small cliff and down she tumbled. After she was pulled up and laid on the ground, first aid was given. She could not walk, so the rescuers improvised a stretcher by putting two long poles through the sleeves of two jackets. She was then carried back to the Island Inn, where she was residing. At the Inn she was checked by a doctor, a visitor to the island, and he found broken bones in one foot and a very badly sprained ankle.

Now I knew why there were shelves of first aid supplies in our pantry. We were not very happy about the way the lady had to be carried, so, requested a stretcher. The Coast Guard sent one post haste. Would you believe, we never used it during our remaining stay on Monhegan?

The Fall season was beautiful, some summer people stayed as long as they could. We had a few cuts and scratches to attend to, but nothing serious. Some were amused to see me use a piece of salt pork on bee or hornet stings. One child thought this worse than the sting.

High on our windy hill (there was almost always a breeze), people loved to sit on our lawn chairs, relax, talk to us, or, just be there. In that case we left them alone. It was very hard to keep Tommy away from them though, and in the end, he most generally ended up talking a blue streak to them. Who could resist an adorable two year old? Well, almost two. His favorite pastime was sitting in Daddy's big chair, looking at *National Geographic* magazines. Of course his knowledge was vast!

Fall was approaching and a ton of work had to be done. Taking down the screens, washing and putting up storm windows, weather stripping doors and windows and on and on. Tons of coal in 50 pound bags and several tanks of propane gas arrived by a Coast Guard Buoy Tender, and had to be trucked up to the lighthouse and properly stowed, our winter supply. We had to batten down the hatches, for we knew not the winters out there. It did seem that we were ten degrees warmer in winter and ten degrees cooler in the summer than it was on the mainland.

When I said "Yes, let's accept a tour of duty at Monhegan Island Light Station," I assumed my days would be filled with just taking care of our son and regular housework. No one told me about inspections by our Commander from Coast Guard Group, Rockland; let alone those by the Commandant, First Coast Guard District, Boston, Massachusetts office; when three officers would arrive to inspect.

Actually, we had to read previous reports prepared by former keepers to find out a lot about our duties. It was like the blind leading the blind, and if we made any mistakes we would find out the hard way.

The buzz word was, "HE would be arriving within the next two weeks." We cleaned, scrubbed and painted until our fingers bled. Well, not quite that bad, but almost. When the fateful day arrived, the "Boys" stationed at Burnt Island L/B/S, gave us a phone call. Bless them, to inform us they were about to head out to Port Clyde, to pick up the Group Commander. That meant we had some warning, time to change our clothes and hold our breath.

From our view atop Lighthouse Hill, we could see them coming, so we could measure the time to get in the truck and drive to the dock to meet them and bring the Commander up to the station for his Inspection. I was peeking out a window when the truck came to a stop outside the house. One look and I thought, here is a man who means business. He's all military and goes by the book. My thoughts were never truer!

First he inspected every out building. He looked over, under, and inside of everything. He pushed, poked and prodded. His pencil was moving fast on his notebook.

Next came the long walkway leading to the light tower, then up the circular stairs and into the lens itself. Putting finger prints on the brasswork as well as the lens prisms, didn't make Ernie very happy. One doesn't say anything, except, "Yes, Sir." or "No, Sir." at times like this. Just grit your teeth and bear it.

Finally, he stated he wanted to see the inside of the house. Oh Boy, it was time for me to hear the military standards of housekeeping.

I stood back as discreetly as possible and watched. He opened cupboard doors, looked under the sink, in the oven and refrigerator. Ran his fingers across the top of the window and door casings, over light bulbs. He looked at, in or under every thing in the whole house. He checked our food supplies. We were to have an extra month's supply on hand at all times. First aid supplies and equipment got a good going over. He examined the coiled ropes tied to each upstairs radiator (in case of fire to be tossed out the window to climb down and escape).

When he decided he had seen enough, he walked into Ernie's office to check the reams of paper work and records that had to be kept. Finally, he wrote in the "Daily Log" book:

"BE EVER SAFETY MINDFUL
BE CAREFUL OF FIRES"

(I heard that comment so much over the years, it is etched on my brain. Even today, I remember and am very careful.)

Our first military inspection was over. I don't recall anything major that we goofed on. I know he found fault with some things, but nothing to demote or transfer us. I do remember we held our breath until we heard the Coast Guard boat leave the dock. Then, and only then did we breath a sigh of relief and collapse with a hot cup of coffee. What was left of the day was spent playing with Tommy. A great way to unwind. Although in the back of our minds was the thought of how we did and when would the next inspection be.

If I thought I was scared when I heard the Group Commander was coming, it doesn't compare to the day I could not find Tommy. One minute he was with me, the next, he was gone. I screamed over the sound of the generator, and Ernie came running to turn it off. There's no need to write all we did and went through, but, I doubt if there are many of you who have looked beyond locked doors, to find something or someone. The one thing we didn't have to worry about, was anyone taking him. We were scared speechless, that Tommy might get the idea of walking away from the house. We stopped hollering, held hands and prayed. Now, calmly, let's just walk around again, and speak Tommy's name.

There he was, sitting and playing in the sand behind the paint locker where we had looked a short time before, talking to himself, living in his own little world. Our knees were so weak, we just sat down beside him and also played in the sand.

Hundreds of times we had told him, when you hear us call for you, just say, "Hear I am!" But, I suppose when you're preoccupied, digging for gold, in some foreign land, it's too far away to hear your parents calling. That was one scare I could have done without. I might add, we heard, "Here I Am" quite often after that.

Christmastime was fast approaching, and I thought it would be nice to spend it with my parents. Ernie put in his leave request papers, and leave was granted. Whenever we left the island, someone had to come to maintain the Light. A relief keeper was sent from Rockland Group and upon his arrival, we departed the island.

We had a happy day, and Santa was good to Tommy. Ernie had to leave the day after Christmas, to return to Monhegan. However, we decided, as my time was nearing, it would be a good idea for me to stay with my parents until the baby was born. Also, if Ernie took only a few days leave now, we hoped he could return when I needed him.

That's exactly the way it happened. He was granted leave again and arrived in Belfast just in time for us to celebrate our six years of marriage. Only thing, I wasn't going to do any dancing this day, 22 January 1957. Shortly after I got Tommy dressed and gave him breakfast, I didn't feel good. So, Ernie took over for the day. Good for father and son to be together, anyway.

The day dragged on. The evening dragggged on. By 10:30 P.M., I had had enough discomfort, so Ernie drove us to the (Old) Waldo County Hospital. Once there, we were informed that the doctor was trying to return to Belfast from Bangor. However, during this January thaw the lowlands and coastal roads were very foggy and he was having a slow, difficult drive.

Just what I needed, a doctor in the fog. In the corner of the waiting room was a comfortable love seat. There we sat, looking at a *Saturday Evening Post* magazine. What a way to spend a wedding anniversary evening. It was also Ernie's 29th birthday!

It wasn't long before the doors swung open, and in flew Dr. Albro. He took one look at me and bellowed, "What in hell are you doing over there?" My reply, "Waiting for you." To which he said, "I thought you so competent, why didn't you go down to the delivery room and have the baby?" While saying this, he grabbed my hand and started pulling me to the delivery room. He told Ernie to hang around, we wouldn't be long.

The hospital was very quiet that late evening, so long as I shut up. Doc even let Ernie come into the delivery room, for a few minutes. I had one sharp pain, grabbed Ernie's upper arm for support and accidentally pinched a nerve. Ernie almost passed out. He asked for some water. The nurse kept saying, "She can't have any." Finally, he said, "It's not for her, it's for me." I don't know if he got the water or not because by then pains were coming so fast the nurse pushed Ernie outside the room and closed the door.

At 12:28 A.M. that morning of January 23rd, 1957, we were celebrating the birth of a beautiful daughter, whom we named Lisa Roxane DeRaps. Sorry Ernie, your birthday present was half an hour late. That's all right, now she will have her own day to celebrate.

When Tommy was born, he had blue eyes, real light colored hair, an olive complexion, weighed 6 lbs. - 14 oz. and was 22 inches long.

Our new daughter was just the opposite. Dark brown hair and eyes and a very pink complexion. She weighed 6 lbs - 3 oz. and was only eighteen and three quarters inches long. Being small boned, Lisa looked even tinier than she really was.

The hospital charged me for a full day, even though I was only there two hours on the 22nd. The total bill was 88 cents less than Tommy's. $30.31. Wish the next eighteen years were as inexpensive.

On the morning of the 27th, Ernie and Tommy came to return us to 25 Miller Street, where Grammie and Grampa were anxiously waiting to welcome us home and to greet their new grand-daughter. After Tommy found out that his sister couldn't play with him, he went back to his toys.

In a week's time, we went to see Dr. Albro and I told him I wanted to return to Monhegan, with Ernie. He said that if I felt up to the trip, go for it. He knew I wouldn't take any chances if I thought anything was wrong. Not having a doctor on the island, makes you think twice about things.

The first week of February, found us returning to our island Lighthouse home on the ferry, *Laura B.* The good Lord, took a liking to us, as the weather was warm and the seas somewhat calm.

In the winter months almost the entire island population came to see the ferry arrive with supplies and the mail. When they saw me and my bundle, a shout of joy and congratulations came from many of them. And, of course, all the ladies had to have a peek at our lovely daughter.

It felt so good to be home, and the relief keeper had kept the house spotless, just as I had left it. After a cup of hot coffee and change of a diaper, we were in business. Being gone a month and a half, Tommy was excited over his old toys, as if they were new. He was happy for days.

A beautiful spring turned into a lovely summer and much company. Dad DeRaps, Ernie's sister Bernadette Muzeroll and her son Peter, my cousins Alice Sanborn and Estelle Baird. I think Mom and Dad made it once. (Ernie seems to think they came by the Coast Guard forty footer. In that case they both must have been at the same place at the same time, going in the same direction. Because they don't ordinarily deal with passengers, out side of military.) All that visited were welcomed, enjoyed the area and got their fill of lobster.

My sister Joan, her husband Bill and their daughter Marie (a year and a half old), visited us the first part of June. Thank the Lord, it was then, while we could enjoy their company and not at the end of the month when we were very busy dealing with a boating accident.

Ah! The end of June, school was out. Summer people were arriving daily. Some to stay all summer in their own cottages, many for a weekend visit and others on daily sight seeing excursions. The majority arrived on the little 65 foot, sea worthy mail-boat *Laura B.* from Port Clyde. Others, mostly on day excursions arrived and departed on the *Balmy Days*, out of Boothbay Harbor.

Ten miles out in the Atlantic, called for something strong and sea-worthy. Even then, Mother Nature might take the situation in hand and give you the surprise of your life.

The days and nights had lengthened into a solid week of constant, thick fog. It was more than annoying, but not unusual for this kind of weather, along or off the coast of Maine.

West of Monhegan, about a tenth of a mile from the dock, was the Coast Guard Fog Signal Station, on Manana Island. Coast Guardsmen attended the radios and fog horn. That noisy horn had been blaring away its warning and would continue until the fog lifted.

We had extinguished the light in the tower at the prescribed time, half an hour after sun rise and covered the lens. Even though the sun wasn't shining, the lens "had to wear her skirt!"

Our two year old son Tommy and our 5 month old daughter, Lisa, had been taken care of for the time being. Ernie was doing some of the constant paperwork the Coast Guard required, and I always had housework to do. Everything was running smoothly. It was a fairly quiet Saturday morning, when the telephone rang.

"Shipwreck at Lobster Cove," a man's voice said excitedly, "You'd better get down there right away!"

Within minutes, my husband was off in the Dodge power wagon, grabbing his foul weather gear from the entry way as he went out the door. I had never been through anything like this before, so hardly knew what to do, but common sense said brew some strong coffee, make sure the first aid kit is handy, even though there was one in the power wagon and get an armload of towels. Any house work not previously done, got a quick going over and I prepared myself for anything and everything.

Not knowing what had happened, or if anyone was hurt, made the waiting almost unbearable. Then, I heard the gears grinding and knew the wagon was laboring up the steep Lighthouse Hill.

Confusion reigned, while we helped six wet, shocked people calm down and towel off. Puddles of water were underfoot, as well as wet clothes, maps and other salvaged boating paraphernalia.

No one was seriously hurt, thank the Lord, just scrapes and bruises. The shock of the accident, plus the cold Atlantic waters, took its toll on everyone. Finally, I persuaded the three women to go upstairs to rest. It was quieter and warmer up there. Two of the men, just paced the floors, trying to calm down. I'm sure they were reliving what had just happened to them. But, the poor Skipper had such a severe headache and was so shaken, that it took hours before any kind of rest came to him.

Piecemeal, I heard the story from those six New Yorkers whom we had welcomed into our home.

They had boarded a sleek, trim, forty-one foot yawl, out of Rye, New York, and sailed for Bar Harbor, Maine. The trip was a joy, until they neared the Maine coast. Fog had set in, "Thick as pea soup!" still all went well until nearly 4 A.M. when the high seas slammed the vessel onto the rocks at Lobster Cove on the southwest promontory of Monhegan.

Two people had been on watch, the others sleeping. In grounding with such force, all were thrown about the craft. Quickly gathering themselves up, they decided they must have landed on a rock pile, somewhere. Not knowing how badly the vessel was damaged, a big decision had to be made. They would try to crawl out onto the rocks. With pounding seas and the yawl listing badly, it was all they could do to stay upright on their feet. After relocating on the rocks, things were just as bad as they were covered with seaweed and continual spray from the pounding seas. Not daring to venture further, they stayed on the rocks.

Not a happy picture. Six frightened people, huddled together for warmth, on hard, cold rocks. Heavy spray keeping them wet. Thick fog obscuring their view. They were shivering from shock as they cared for their cuts, bruises and sprains as best they could.

It was 7 A.M. before there was enough light and the visibility improved enough for them to see they were on rocks off a headland. After three long hours, huddled together on the rocks with the tide getting higher every minute, giving them less and less to stay on, it was a great relief to scramble to a patch of grass and higher ground. Many prayers were said and answered.

All day long, numerous attempts were made to remove the yawl from its rocky bed. After every try, the raging sea pushed the craft further aground, until it could no longer be floated.

Such a sorry sight to see. By late afternoon, one side was breaking up, the once beautiful mahogany deck battered, the stainless steel galley all awash. Everything inside was floating; new linens, clothes, bedding, etc. Very little was saved, but the people were, thank God. They will get over their ordeal; yawls can be built and replaced, but people cannot!

The six stayed with us for the week-end, and by Monday were well enough to return to New York City, hoping to see Monhegan again, but under different circumstances!

We salute: Nancy, Joan, Ellen, Robert, Frank and Richard, and will remember them always. All six signed a paper for us. I like what Richard wrote, "A hospitable port in a storm, is a wonderful thing. Thanks for all." and Joan wrote, "The DeRaps make Monhegan a pleasant memory, in spite of how we got here."

Our daily living went back to normal. We enjoyed every minute of our tour of duty on Monhegan Island. Never forgetting that exciting weekend in June, nor the people we tried to comfort.

They say, modernization is progress. Sometimes, I wonder, and specially when it concerns automating the lights on lighthouses.

That summer of '57, we were hearing that Monhegan Light Station would be closing. The light would be automated. I couldn't believe it; "Not Monhegan," I whined. "They can't do it to a light that is needed as much as this one. Progress, my foot. I don't believe it."

This light has been standing guard for over one hundred years. Marine pilots came and still come to Monhegan and board ships from all over the world and navigate them up Penobscot Bay to the docks of Searsport, and up the Penobscot River to Bucksport and the head of tide at Bangor. Men who knew the importance of the lights have stated, "Lighthouses should be manned. Sometimes there are accidents and people are needed to take care of the situation. No automated Lighthouse can pull someone up off the cliffs if they fall, nor can it take care of people who are shipwrecked. No automated lighthouse can save a human life, nor can it help fishermen who run aground, or capsize, or run out of gas or need help for any number of reasons. Lighthouses should be manned by people." When a Lighthouse is abandoned, it often falls victim to vandalism. Stations that the United States Government have laid out thousands upon thousands of dollars for upkeep. Unless some concerned people and/or business organizations, or societies raise monies to care for these beautiful, old, historical, needed, Lighthouses; they will be torched, vandalized, smashed, dismantled or left for Mother Nature to destroy.

THIS SHOULD NOT HAPPEN.

I will not bore you further with my tirade about saving Lighthouses. Today, we all know what has happened. Suffice to say, we were the last FAMILY to live in the Lighthouse on Monhegan. One wonderful thing happened out there. A group of people gathered together and bought the dwelling. Monhegan Associates have made a museum there. Thank God for them. Now, if the government will loosen up and let others do the same thing in their area and stop fighting them, maybe more Lighthouses can be saved. I certainly pray that happens!

Andrew George Winter, born in Estonia in 1892, came to the United States in 1916 at the age of 24. In 1921 he became a naturalized U.S. citizen. He received his artistic schooling in New York City. He was a self taught artist until he entered the free art school of the National Academy of design in 1925, where he won a scholarship for a year of art study abroad.

Sea scenes were etched in his mind, from more than 15 years of traveling on freighters, ocean liners, fishing schooners and army transports. Each summer, he had to give up his painting, regretfully, and ship before the mast for several months to earn enough to live on while he continued with his paintings and drawings.

His Maine seascapes won him international fame. He was listed in 'Who's Who in America," was included in the New York World's Fair of 1940 for an outstanding contribution in the field of art by an American citizen of foreign birth. Reprints of Mr. Winter's paintings, were in the 1958 issue of *Ford Times*, published by Ford Motor Co. Over the years, he won many awards.

In 1928, while at the Academy of Design, he married a student, Mary Taylor, and they lived in New York City. In the 1930's they showed their work at the National Academy, Chicago Art Institute and the Tiffany Foundation.

After making many winter trips to Monhegan so Andrew could paint its rugged scenery during the coldest part of the year, they moved to Monhegan in 1942, permanently.

It wasn't long before the public found where Andy lived and they beat a path to his upstairs studio in his home. Afraid the flooring wouldn't hold many people, he and Mary built a studio, with a large north window for light and a huge stone fireplace for heat. This was above where their house stood on lower Lighthouse Hill.

Andrew became ill, early 1958 and on 27 October that year died at age 66, in Brookline, Maine. He left his lovely wife, Mary, and a brother August of Estonia. Private funeral services were held and burial was at his special painting area, on the South side of Monhegan called White Head Cliffs. Here his ashes were strewn over the cliffs and waters of his beloved Monhegan.

We, Ernie and I, like to remember Andy, tall and vibrant, and teasing his wife when we four played cribbage, winter nights in 1956. It was relaxing for them and got Ernie away from the constant paperwork, that had to be done.

One day, after Andy finished the studio fireplace, he needed help putting a cap over the chimney. Ernie was more than glad to help and Andy wanted to pay him for the work. On being told government workers could not take money, Andy said nothing. A few days later, there was a knock on our door, there stood Andy with a large, paper wrapped package. "Here", he said, "I want you to have this, and, don't say you can't accept it." We are the proud owners of one Andrew Winter painting.

Mrs. Andrew Winter, known to the painting world as Mary Taylor, always had a smile to go with her sparkling personality. Her dark, thick hair looked like it would topple her tiny framed body.

Mary started out using water colors when in high school, but, switched to oils when at the Cummings School of Art in Des Moines, in her native Iowa. She majored in art at Iowa University and was art supervisor for the schools of Fort Morgan, Colorado, before coming east. Wanting to go to New York, she entered the school of National Academy of Design in New York City. There she met and married the handsome Andrew Winter. The rest is history.

Mary painted on small canvases, using vibrant colors of red, yellow, orange and so forth. Clear and true colors made her paintings almost come to life.

After Andy died, she stayed in the studio and sold their home. Winters she lived in a trailer in Florida, not being very happy with the cold of Maine.

All the people we met on Monhegan, were very interesting, whether they lived there or came to visit. Author, Ida Sedgwick Proper, lived down the hill. She wrote a very interesting book called, *Monhegan, The Cradle of New England*, printed by The Southworth Press; Portland, Maine in 1930. Ida was a small lady we would see walking along with her Collie dog, taking their daily stroll to the post office. Professors from McGill University of Canada, to the hard working lobstermen, everyone, we found special. And we will never forget our stay at Monhegan.

I'll relate one incident of the friendliness of the island people. A very short time after we had moved to Monhegan, Ernie was at the store one day and made the acquaintance of one of the lobstermen. He asked if we liked lobsters. On being told affirmative, plus, he stated he would see what he could do. A date was set and one evening, Donnie, his wife and four children arrived with two huge buckets full of the most beautiful lobsters you ever saw. Our long dining room table was the scene of one of the most delicious meals I ever had, and delightful company finished the evening.

One beautiful fall afternoon, while the children were taking their nap, I went outside and sat in one of the two summer chairs; most generally used by the summer visitors, vacated now because the visitors were all gone.

Enjoying the warm sunshine and the peace and quiet, I contemplated all I surveyed; the lovely village was still, as if all the inhabitants were taking a nap. The glimmer of the sun shone on the ocean, sliding just across the tips of waves which were small ripples. No telling what the wind would be doing to the water in the next few minutes. Over on Manana Island, the only sound came from the sheep the hermit owned.

I haven't mentioned anything about Ray, have I? He did not look like my idea of a hermit, actually, when he cleaned up and put on street clothes, you would never believe he spent most of his time living on the cliffs of an island. He was a quiet, nice looking man. A former chemical engineer from New York City who decided, during the great depression, to retreat to a life of solitude on a craggy rock 10 miles at sea. His many small buildings home was put together from boards, gathered from the rocks as well as from people on Monhegan who had no further use for them. His sheep came out on the mail-boat; that must have been a sight to see. And, picture the hermit taking them from Monhegan in his open boat and rowing them over to Manana. That must have been something to watch. He made his pen money by selling the wool.

Ray the hermit, took two or three trips to the mainland each year. One time he went to the Gaspe and ended up skiing. So you see, he didn't completely hibernate.

Back to my thoughts . . . . I would never forget my first, but not last wild sea ride. I call it "My first and last Atlantic run" as we never returned to Monhegan after we left.

That trip, plus living on the island, taught me a lot. For one thing, those Coast Guardsmen, really knew how to handle their crafts in any kind of weather. I had and still have a great amount of pride and respect for them. Not a milquetoast in that group.

The people who lived year around on Monhegan Island, are a special class of people. Independent, hard workers, who make their livelihood from the sea, by lobstering. And that was special too. If everyone was ready, and only then, Trap Day, was New Year's Day. That was the day when all the men stacked all the traps they could get on their boats, then went out and set them in their designated area. No matter the weather. I have seen them go out in weather that wasn't fit for a fish. Seas so high you lost sight of man and boat in the waves. And watching from my high perch, in the living room, the rough seas looked even more menacing. The men were called the highest paid lobstermen in the world. Let me tell you, they earned every cent they made by just going to sea, never mind their hauling up lobsters that were the best.

Even though the ferry almost always ran on schedule, there were days when you'd not want to make use of its services because of the terrible weather conditions. There were a few times, when the skipper Mr. Fields said, "No, we don't go today! No sense in taking chances of lost lives, supplies or the vessel. That sea is too strong for my little 65 footer, today."

Your only other connection with the mainland was the telephone, of which there were three. One at the store, one at the post office and at the Lighthouse which was used for government matters only or in an emergency. Therefore, in sixteen months, I never made a phone call, not one.

With no resident doctor, on the island, you worked at staying healthy and used every preventative to stay that way. We did have to make one fast trip to the main, when Tommy scratched his eyeball on a toy. We didn't dare take a chance, to see if it would heal by itself. So, another 40 footer C. G. boat ride. They were even kind enough to have a pickup truck waiting for us to use to go to Belfast to see our doctor. After he checked the eye, put in an ointment and put on a patch to be left on until we were back on the island. We were in luck again, no real harm done, except, Tommy did an awful lot of strutting around to show off his patch.

With no roads to amount to, travel was by foot. There were a few trucks to haul supplies from the dock to the store, mail to the post office and lobster traps from home to the wharf.

Monhegan was a great place to be, providing you could cope with a semi-solitary existence. That you didn't have to be on the go all the time, shopping for food or clothes, visiting the beauty parlor, go out for entertainment, or want to travel all over the place.

A lot of people commented; "How do you survive living up here, never able to leave when you want to? Don't you get bored? Aren't you lonely? No way could I stand it for month after month. Doubt if I'd last two days!"

My answer was always the same. I guess it takes a special breed to stay and enjoy this kind of living. First of all, I'm not alone. I have my husband. We like each other and being together. (Although when my Irish temper gets out of hand, he will be long gone away from me; doing chores, down to the village getting the mail, changing the oil in the truck, or maybe out counting pieces of coal left in the bin!)

I have two children to care for which takes considerable time. One is a baby and the other needs constant watching, making sure he stays very near the house.

But, people wanted to know what you did in your FREE time. Well, we had a tiny television, that we seldom watched. We played a lot of cribbage, some games, put jigsaw puzzles together. My main free time occupation was reading. I adore books. Even today, a new edition of Phillis A. Whitney, Eugenia Price, Siddons, Michener, or Terry C. Johnston, with his Indian or wild west stories, just to name a few, will send me scurrying to get my housework done, so that I can find a quiet corner to read and get lost.

We have dozens of books about Maine. I have seen potato blossoms in Aroostook County, the Blueberry Barrens downeast, the mineral mines in Oxford County and been to L.L. Bean's. But, it's nice to read about the other places so highly advertised.

I have three shelves full of beautiful books about Ireland. With any one of them in my lap, I'm sent dreaming of my ancestors homeland. I've always stated, "If you have a good book, you are never lonesome!"

So, my family, my daily activities, and books, made my life most enjoyable. Plus, always being prepared for unexpected happenings, keeps you on tippy-toes.

I don't recall being bored or lonesome while we did our tour of duty on lovely Monhegan Island. In fact, days would come, years later, when I would have given just about everything I owned, to once again, enjoy a warm, breezy, quiet afternoon, with the sea all around me; on Monhegan.

Beginning with ten, small, armed boats; authorized by the first U.S. Congress, on August 4, 1790, to guard the nation's coasts from smuggling and to enforce maritime and custom laws - we have the United States Coast Guard. In 1832, the Secretary of the Treasury ordered several Revenue Cutters to cruise the Atlantic coast and give protection to ships during the winter. This winter cruising was made part of the regular duties of the Cutter Service until radio communications made it unnecessary. Known first as the Revenue Marine, later, Revenue Cutter Service, and officially combined with the Lifesaving Service on January 28, 1915, to be called the United States Coast Guard (U.S.C.G). The Lighthouse Service established in 1789 under federal control, was consolidated with the U.S.C.G. in 1939. The Lighthouse Service employees were allowed to keep their distinctive uniforms and positions under the Coast Guard consolidation, until such time as they reached retirement. The Bureau of Marine Inspection and Navigation was put under Coast Guard jurisdiction in 1942.

The previous paragraph is just a little bit of information, tucked in, because when we were transferred to our next duty station, the former keeper was one of the last of the Lighthouse Service people on duty under the Coast Guard.

We received word, the first week of December 1957; that Mr. Ernest Mathie of the Lighthouse Service and keeper of Fort Point Lighthouse at Cape Jellison; Stockton Springs, Maine, had passed away on the third of the month. We were assigned to become the first Coast Guard personnel to be stationed there.

Fort Point Light Station

I certainly was not very pleased to be moving in the month of December, plus, right before the holidays, but, I felt much sympathy for Mrs. Mathie, so kept quiet of my feelings. Here was the dear lady, who had spent the past decade, living with her own furnishings, and her husband in the close quarters of lighthouse living, now, she had to plan his funeral, move furniture and self out of her safe haven. They had a nice little home in Belfast, they planned to move to, in the summer of 1958, when the Mr. was to retire. Ah, the fates of life!

A relief keeper stayed at Fort Point Lighthouse, to tend the light, and fog bell if needed. Someone had to be there to assist, when the government brought in a complete house full of new furnishings. I was thrilled with everything, and ready to use my cleaning expertise, except, when I saw the couch! It was white leatherette. White? With two small children? They did very well though, the couch was as white when we left as when we moved in.

One week before Christmas, the 16th of December to be exact, we said good-by to Monhegan Island. It must have been a good trip, because I don't remember anything exciting happening. Maybe, I was so relieved to return to the mainland, and be able to see my parents, friends and go shopping, once in awhile without taking a ferry.

Christmas Eve, we were all set for the big man to show. House decorated, tree up, and presents under it. Every thing was in its place. Again, I knew I was going to like living here. New Years Eve, we rolled up the rugs and had a party. My parents, Tom and Jennie and my sister Anita and her husband Dean, arrived. We even danced through the living and dining rooms. Welcome 1958, "What will you have in store for us??".

Another party on the 22nd for Ernie's 30th birthday, (as well as our 7th wedding anniversary) and the next day, our little daughter Lisa would be one year old.

The month of February, we sort of rested and got acquainted with the neighborhood, our new duties and the lay of the land. We knew by the first of March, and for the next eight months, we would be busy cleaning, painting, and being ready for those "unexpected" inspections.

Fort Point Lighthouse was built in 1836 and re-built in 1857, the tower was square on the outside, while round inside. The light was 88 feet above the water. Near the house was a small building for supplies like lawn mowers, rakes and such and an emergency standby generator. The generator was to be used for the tower light, when the commercial power failed. About 300 yards from the dwelling was the end of Penobscot Bay and the beginning of the Penobscot River. About 300 feet south of the buildings was a thirty foot drop off into 90 feet of water. Follow a long wooden walkway Northeast and you came to the bell tower (fog signal). When needed, you heard 1 stroke every 20 seconds. Oh my, this is interesting. To keep the bell dinging, two thousand pounds of weights had to be wound up. Now, that is exercise for you. We got smart very fast and did our winding after the weights were down half way. Better to wind for ten minutes, than twenty!

I forgot to mention, the light had 4500 candle power and could be seen 15 miles, and, the light was on the west side of the mouth of the river.

The next twenty-two months were to be the best years of our lives, up to then. It was a grand tour of duty. Nothing major happened, just a lot of little things, made life very nice.

We hadn't been at this station very long before we had our first inspection by our Group

Commander, Mr. Litchfield. After he saw how I kept house, I never saw him again. He would arrive, check the grounds, light tower, out buildings, and paper work. Leave his message; like they all did, "Be Ever Safety Mindful, Be Careful of Fires!" Then he'd leave. We were always ready for inspection, so actually didn't mind his arrival.

One time when Ernie asked if he wanted to inspect the inside of the house, our Commander laughingly stated, "I'm not going in there and maybe dirty her floor. She'd no doubt give me hell." I wonder what traveled faster - news about my clean house or my Irish disposition. ' I have a sign in my room — "WARNING, disposition subject to change without notice!"

Now when the District sent three men, that was a different story. We were on pins and needles for days. One inspector would stay with Ernie, one with me, and the other would look around. I used to call it snooping, because nobody would be with him, and he could go where he pleased. By the time the inspection was over, each man had been with Ernie, me and did his "snooping" by himself. I recall this was the one time I blew a fuse, after they had left.

In inspecting the house, they had gone upstairs, and in the process had woken Tommy and Lisa from their naps. Not only did that get my goat, they looked in the closets, and even the dresser drawers. I was livid. I wished there had been a rubber bra that would have bounced up and hit them in the face. My Gawd, wasn't there anything sacred? Couldn't we have a place they didn't have to see? I made such a stink, Ernie promised me when the Group Commander came again, he would ask if it was necessary for the inspectors to go into our bedrooms. I made sure the question was asked, you can bet on that. Lo and behold!! Would you believe, they were NOT supposed to enter the upstairs. That was considered our private property, while on a government reservation. You can bet again, I never got fooled again. And, the time did arise, at another station, when we had three men from Boston (District Headquarters), who tried to go upstairs and inspect. I stopped them cold, at the bottom step. This time they were livid. I spent the rest of the day, giggling and thinking I had gotten away with murder. I was so pleased with myself. Hey! They knew the rules, they just didn't think the rest of us knew. Strange how some will take advantage of you, when they think you're helpless.

At Monhegan, we asked for and received the needed stretcher. At Fort Point, we asked for and received fencing for an area for the children to play. With a thirty feet drop into ninety or so feet of water, I thought it was needed. For my peace of mind, if nothing else. Also, if we had company, and they had children, it would help them too. Of course, the government was too poor to send nice fencing, we received snow fencing, instead. It did the job, and we were thankful.

A long time ago in the nearby woods, stood a huge hotel, it burned at the turn of the 20th century, leaving nothing but bricks. The land was owned by a neighbor, Mr. Costello, who donated some bricks to Mr. Mathie, the former keeper, to make an outdoor fireplace in the summer of 1952.

The summer of 1958, we put that nice fireplace to work, cooking the most delicious meals, for the most delightful company anyone could have, namely my parents, my sisters and their families, Ernie's Dad, his sister Bernadette and son Peter. I even remember Merle and Doreen being there once. They were the parents of my brother-in-law, Dean. In-laws or out laws, it didn't matter. It was a summer for week-end picnics, from noon 'til midnight.

We must have behaved ourselves, cause we never heard from our neighbors; the Foster's, Costello's, Sanborn's or the delightful Wardwell's. Most of them only stayed for the summer, and no doubt were having their own fun and parties.

We were given permission to have a garden, the summers of '58 and '59. That was the best dirt we had played in for some time. The veggies grew like crazy. We even grew a two pound potato that kept Ernie eating for a meal or two, seeing he loves spuds so much and could eat them for every meal. I didn't grow any beyond my hundred pounds of wonder, that summer, but I sure got a tan being outdoors so much. That and my short haircut made me look like I should have been out in the woods or down by the shore, grinding corn.

Another permission granted Ernie, was to help Boy Scout Troop 235, sponsored by the Jerry W. Dobbins American Legion Post No. 157 of Stockton Springs and Prospect. It takes Ernie to tell the whole story about Scouting, but, I can state one summer they wanted a Camporee and needed tents for which they had no money. Ernie said, "We will make them ourselves." Everyone thought he was crazy, so with my old treadle sewing machine, Ernie made a tent, water proofed it and proved it could be done. After all was said and done, about twelve Explorer type tents were made, used and kept everyone dry. Ernie got me into the act, making neckerchiefs. I did the cutting, sewing, etc. and he painted the theme on about three dozen. Just something to keep our hands active, that's all.

On the 10th of January 1959, we saw a small vessel coming up the bay. It was the *Sunbeam*, from the Maine Seacoast Missionary Society; out of Bar Harbor, Maine. Tommy grabbed the rope, gave it a good tug and rang the fog signal bell to welcome them. They anchored near Number One river buoy and rowed a small boat ashore. We had a lovely visit, plus tea and cookies.

Sunbeam III, was 72 feet long - diesel powered and the fifth vessel in succession which since 1905 have been dedicated to practical Christian Service along the coast of Maine. Maintained by contributions; owned and operated by the Maine Seacoast Mission Society. During their visit the Reverend Neal Bousfield distributed belated Christmas gifts to our children. This is another of their lovely attributes.

Another exciting happening back then was the Flying Santa Claus. Author, Edward Rowe Snow, who wrote about the New England coastline and Naval History, for forty years, flew up and down the coast dropping Christmas bundles at Lighthouses and remote military installations. Talk about excitement!!

We would hear through the grape vine, when Santa would be flying our area to drop his bundle, sure enough, out of the clouds came the little Cessna. The package landed down over the hill, and it was exciting to wave to him and retrieve the goodies. Always a book, which satisfied me, mittens and a toy for the children. What a beautiful gesture, and what a thrill it must have been for those who lived on remote places.

Dear Edward Rowe Snow at the age of 79, passed beyond the clouds, the 10th of April, 1982. I'll bet he is still bringing good will to all!

>> — <<

There was a well placed window over the sink in the kitchen I could see across the driveway into a field, that for some reason unbeknown to me, was fenced off. One day as I was doing the dishes, I gasped in surprise, as a deer was attempting to jump over the fence. On closer look, I couldn't believe what I saw. I ran to get Ernie, to come out in the kitchen and have him verify the scene. Sure enough, the deer had only three legs. One front leg was completely gone. Try after try she strived to jump the fence. Finally she succeeded, I don't know who was the more exhausted, her or us. We have never forgotten that beautiful creature's endurance and perseverance. We also wonder how she lost her leg.

I believe I have stated before, just below the bell tower, in the water was Number One river buoy. This designated the end of the bay and the mouth of the Penobscot River. River traffic was mostly small oil tankers and freighters going upriver to Bucksport or Bangor, Maine. Actually, we don't know what was carried, as you couldn't see their cargo. In the winter the ice breakers would pass by if needed up the river.

All foreign vessels coming into state or federal waters must have a licensed Maine pilot on board. We knew two of these pilots; Abbott and Gamashe. They liked nothing better than playing tricks on us. Very late at night or about two in the morning when we were sleeping. They would pilot the ship as close as they could to the house and shine their search lights on the upper story, which just so happened to be our bedroom. As if that wasn't enough, they would blast away on their horns and sirens. They certainly got our attention. It broke up the monotony.

Now, I must tell you how Polly pulled the 'Boo Boo' of the century. Here at Fort Point Lighthouse, as well as Monhegan, the flag was raised every morning at eight o'clock, saluted; and then we started the day in earnest. No pun, intended. Ernie most generally did the honors. But one windy, cold morning he was busy and I said I would do it. I had an awful time raising the flag because the wind was whipping around the corner, and the flag around me. Finally, I succeeded to get it to the top, wound the rope around the cleat and ran into the house, half frozen. I never gave the flag a look or thought about it again.

River traffic was zero that day, until about three in the afternoon, when a small tanker went down the bay. It was still in sight when the telephone rang and a voice bellowed, "What's the problem?" I couldn't imagine who it was, or what they were talking about. And, wouldn't you know, Ernie was not at the station to take care of business. It was up to me to address the problem, if there was any.

Again, the question was asked, "What's your problem?" and I stated there was nothing wrong here. "Well," the voice continued. "This is the Coast Guard Base Rockland calling, and you have a distress signal flying. We have the Coast Guard Cutter on her way up to your place, as well as the forty-footer, a plane out of Salem, Massachusetts" and he went on and on. I was aghast as I took our Lighthouse duties very serious and never wanted any mistakes.

In my hysteria I thought, "My God, it sounds like the whole Coast Guard Command are coming to our rescue." I was about to lose it, when I noticed there was silence on the other end of the line. Now the voice said very calmly, "Polly, is the flag flying upside down? Go outside and check it, and take care of it, NOW. You know that is a sign of distress. And, by the way, nothing is on its way to your place. I was just kidding; but, don't let it happen again!"

I knew who was on the other end of the call, now. I recognized his voice and when he said he was only kidding about all of the assistance en route, I could have bopped him on the nose, if he were near. Putting me through the hell he did. After I thought about it for a while, I was glad it was someone I knew, for a horrible mistake had been made.

From that day till this, if I put up a flag; I don't care if a Siberian express wind storm is blowing - I LOOK UP to the flag to see that it is flying properly. I took full blame for the error, and said it was my fault. I was scared to death that Ernie would get in trouble for my actions. I could not have that. Nothing further was ever said about the incident. Phew!! A hard lesson, well learned.

After re-living through my blunder, I have to relax and write about something quiet. Even though we lived down a long dirt road, all alone, with the nearest neighbors up the road a ways; there were days when I needed to be by myself. Alone! I loved my husband and my two children, but, being constantly in or near the house, would get to me after a while.

Down at the point of land, a comfortable distance from the house, was a big birch tree, just standing there, waiting for someone to sit down and lean against it and relax. That is where you would find me, rejuvenating myself. I never took a book, or paper and pen. Just myself, strolling along, enjoying the fresh air, peace and solitude. I might sit there for half an hour, leaning against my favorite kind of tree, or sometimes, I might lay down and watch the clouds float by. The main thing was, it did me a world of good, and when I returned back to the house, things seemed better. I visited my "contemplation tree" from spring to late fall. Ernie always knew where to find me.

There are all kinds of aids to navigation; lighthouses, lightships, daybeacons, buoys and fog signals, just to name a few. At Fort Point Light Station, we had a fog signal bell. A pretty little thing that hung on the outside of the bell tower. I believe a Paul Revere brand, weighing about a THOUSAND pounds. Inside the tower was the mechanics to make it work. The sound came from a hammer actuated by a descending weight of about a ton. Each signal has its own characteristics, ours was a stroke every 20 seconds.

It was a great invention, when it worked well, and when it didn't it wasn't reliable. Our worse case was a solid month of fog. Day after day, night after night, the bell rang until something happened and it stopped. For thirty-six hours, Ernie worked on that blasted machine, to no avail. Finally, he couldn't stay awake any longer, and asked me to take over.

Did you ever attempt to fix something, while trying to ring a bell three times a minute? It's almost impossible. The fog was so thick, when you stepped outside it enveloped you. You were soaking wet if you stayed out very long. The bell tower was a good distance from the house. After walking a few feet away, I couldn't see a darn thing. I had to grope my way down a long boardwalk, hanging onto a rope. Scared to death! This time I even carried a heavy wrench, for protection. Good grief, if I had ever swung that thing, no doubt it would have sent me over the railing and into the waters below. I just prayed there were no ships in the vicinity.

I am about as mechanical minded as a frog. What in the world did Ernie think I could do to keep the bell ringing, I couldn't imagine, though he had tried to teach me. I couldn't see myself standing there the rest of the night, making a gong sound every 20 seconds. Or to almost freeze in the cold, damp, foggy air; and I forgot to bring a thermos of hot tea or coffee.

To make a long night a short story, would wonders never cease, I got the bell working all by itself about three A.M. After four hours of trying, I was exhausted, cold and tired, but elated. (Gee! Long ago, when I learned to repair clocks and watches at Kann's Dept. Store; must have come in handy after all.)

We lived in Government quarters, we abided by military rules and Mother Nature's whims. It's with permission and our ability that we are where we are. We like it here, so strive to go beyond our best in doing all we have to do. Whether it be keeping a spotless house, ready for inspection at a minutes notice, grooming the grounds, making sure all buildings are cleaned, painted, and everything in its place. Brasswork polished, windows gleaming, paper work kept up to the minute. There was always something that had to be started, worked on and finished. Never enough hours in a day to do all that had to be done. You worked six days a week. On the seventh, you collapsed. It was your day of rest to do as you saw fit.

We loved where we were, Fort Point Lighthouse. We were adult enough to accept the rules we had to live by. Actually, being and staying on schedule was a help not a hindrance. Living our secluded life agreed with us, and our living constantly together, wasn't so bad either. When we got tired of each other, I walked to my tree, or Ernie went for a nature walk. It worked every time. (Still does!)

I don't want you to think we never had company, except on Sundays. It was a treat when our Sea and Shore Warden or Game Warden arrived—at times together. Some times with a box of doughnuts. (We had the coffee and tea!) They kept us up-to-date on state affairs, and where the best fishing was, although Ernie seldom went.

The mailman was our daily visitor, he kept us posted on town happenings. So, you see we were kept abreast of town, state and government news, quite often.

I have always been interested in history. Down on Cape Jellison peninsula, it overflowed.

About 25 steps from the back door of the dwelling, — flowed the accumulated waters of the longest river in Maine, the Penobscot. Three hundred and fifty miles long. the west branch rises near the Canadian frontier, flows east and south-east, to where it meets the east branch of the Penobscot river. Afterwards, the course is south-southwest to the Penobscot Bay, then on to the Atlantic Ocean. It is tidal and navigable for large vessels to Bangor, sixty miles from it's mouth here at Fort Point.

Walk about seventy steps north from the same doorway, and you will see a granite marker stating:

FORT POWNAL

Erected and named by

General Thomas Pownal   1759

General Samuel Waldo,

for whom Waldo County was named,

was buried here.

Removed to King's Chapel, Boston

Erected by John Cocran Chapter D. A. R.   1916

Beyond this marker, one sees what is left of the famous Fort Pownal; which 200 plus years ago, was bursting with activity. Nothing remains except the old well, bricks from the chimneys, mounds of earth showing the outline of the forts breastworks and moat. After a rain storm the moat sometimes holds water which freezes during the winter. The drawbridge faced south, where now stands Fort Point Lighthouse. You can see where the drawbridge used to be by an indentation in the earth.

When doing the dishes, I'd gaze out the kitchen window, across the driveway and into the field and fort area, trying to visualize the life of long ago.

We made the acquaintance of Alice V. Ellis, who lived in the nearby village of Stockton Springs, and learned she had written a book in 1955 called *The Story of Stockton Springs, Maine*. The book was written in conjunction with the town's Historical Society and printed by the Kelly Press of Belfast, Maine (where Ernie once worked).

After reading about the Indians, the British and the Fort of 1759; one should read: *The Penobscot Expedition*, by John E. Cayford. An account of the largest American naval engagement of the Revolutionary War. The ill-fated American armada of almost 40 ships, the majority ended up on the bottom of the Penobscot River in 1779.

A little over a hundred years later, beyond where the Fort had stood; a huge hotel was built (about 1890). An old newspaper clipping reads: "It was almost rectangular in shape, with a high basement, three stories and a mansard roof relieved by a high tower. Wide verandas surrounded the buildings first and second floors.

Its interior was magnificent, finish and furnishings lavish. No expense was spared. There were accommodations for two hundred people to stroll the broad verandas, vast stretches of hall and corridors, bowling alley and a billiard room.

The fireplaces and foundations were made from Mount Waldo granite. The lawns and flower beds were beautiful and spacious.

Beside the hotel; was a gas plant which furnished lights for the buildings, buildings for the hired help and stables for horses and ponies. Later an octagon shaped dance hall was built.

Carriages were run daily to the village and the mail was delivered in a sealed pouch.

The first name was, The Wassaumkeag Hotel, then changed to Fort Point House, The Woodcliff and finally Fort Point Hotel.

The first years it was the resort of the elite. Socially prominent promenaded the verandas, feasted on the most elaborate menus served by trained New York waiters and danced to the music of the best orchestras of the day.

A poster advertised the 125 room hotel as, "Handsomely furnished, with gas, salt and fresh water baths, billiard room, has livery stable and bowling alleys, delightful scenery, pleasant drives, fine sailing and fishing and telegraph connection."

About this time, people were starting to learn about Bar Harbor. That it was an even better place to wine and dine, and live. So, after being sold and resold, the owners getting poorer and poorer, the end came on the night of 7 June 1898; when all the buildings burned to the ground.

On the 14th of July, 1959; we were visited by a lovely 91 year old lady named Miss Marion Webster. She was a delight to talk with and we learned that

Miss Webster was born in Orland, Maine on the 20th of May, 1868. Her family moved to Bucksport and stayed there until she was eight years old. Then they moved to Blue Hill Bay Lighthouse for five years.

About 1880, and for the next 20 years, her family lived at Fort Point Lighthouse. One time her father fell and broke many ribs so she had to leave her studies at East Main Seminary to come home and tend the light.

Miss Marion had this to say about the hotel burning. "It was a lovely, calm and quiet evening. My father, Adelbert Webster, then the keeper of Fort Point Light, was going about his work, when all of a sudden, he noticed that the Fort Point Hotel was on fire. No telephones then, his only way of calling for help, was by ringing the fog bell — everyone knew the fog bell wouldn't be needed this clear night, so its ringing meant trouble on the point. By the time the horse drawn fire wagon arrived the hotel was beyond saving. Work was turned to saving the lighthouse. Inside, Mrs. Webster and children were packing clothes and things they wanted to save, in case they had to vacate. Fortunately, it turned out they didn't have to leave!

We later learned that Miss Webster started a teaching career at the age of 15, teaching at the Sandy Point Elementary. She later taught 15 years in Indiana, then on to Williams School in Chelsea, Massachusetts and at North Adams Training School, Principal in Tewksbury, Massachusetts and Head of the Geography Department at Fitchburg Teachers College.

She attended Bridgewater Normal School, University of Maine and Radcliffe. She gained her Bachelor and Master Degrees of science after accepting a teaching position at Horace Mann School at Columbia University, earning her degrees in two years. A college Professor for 16 years, she retired in 1939.

She loved to read Pearl Buck, Twain and Kipling, and read at least eight to ten books a week.

Before I finish this saga about the hotel, I want to tell of my finding while wandering around the grounds where the old building had been.

On one of my afternoon jaunts about the fort, I decided to walk over where the hotel had been. The years of wind and rain had done a pretty good job of covering the burned area with leaves and ground shifts and time, but you still could kick into a brick or mound of something. This day, I decided to do some scratching in the earth, don't ask me why I wanted to dig up this spot, I just wanted to. Much to my surprise, I unearthed what felt like metal on the tines of my little fork. After brushing and digging out the dirt, I could see I had found something. I believe it's pewter, and the top of a butter dish. After more rubbing, I read the words, "Fort Point Hotel" on the side of the cover. I smoothed my diggings over and flew back to the Lighthouse with my find, as excited as a child!

Belfast, Maine; being my hometown I grew up reading, seeing and learning about the whole area. So of course the Penobscot River and Bay are my favorites. When I was a kid, once in a while we would go down to the shore with the family and have a clam bake. Clams, cooked in seaweed taste the best, plus some salt water. Later years, my girlfriend and I would go down to the city park (on the Bay), for a picnic or just to stroll around. One winter we went down and smart ass me, sat on a cake of ice to have my picture taken. I have the picture all right, but Louise forgot to take the best photo of me, when the ice broke and started drifting away from the pack. She was so scared she started running away, leaving unswimable me to fend for myself. It was tricky, but I'm sitting here, so guess I made it. They didn't call me "Tomboy Polly" for nothing.

Getting back to the Cape Jellison area. Ah! Don't I wish I were there. I really loved that place, and wished I could live there forever, near the waters of my favorite river with history all around me. I could ramble off dates of the Indian Wars, all about the British building the Fort, the Americans sinking their own ships in the Revolutionary War, the Hotel. Anything I found Historical that happened on or about the Cape, I talked about. Not forgetting the secluded and protected cove out back of the point where in sailing days, hundreds of ships would moor for cover in gale winds. I finally got Ernie interested in all this.

We thought this a great area for a State Park. I could share my favorite spot with others. We talked with neighbors and they thought the idea was a good one.

With letters and phone calls, we like to think we had something to do in making our thoughts turn to reality.

In April of 1966, the Governor's Executive Council authorized the State Parks and Recreation Commission to purchase a 175 acre tract of land on Cape Jellison, Stockton Springs; to be used for a park and recreational area. The property, adjacent to the lighthouse, Fort Pownal Memorial including more than a mile of shore, would have potential for boaters as well as tourists and residents, using U.S. Routes One and Three.

Today, Fort Point State Park is a lovely place to visit and we go there every chance we can. We hope you visit the area, especially, if you have never been there. In June 1988, Fort Point Light Station was entered in the National Register of Historical places, which means the property is worthy of preservation and protection.

Heron Neck Light Station

I was heart sick when I heard we were being transferred in October 1959, that the station would soon be automated and no one would live in the lighthouse. Little did I realize exactly twenty nine years would pass before that would actually happen. Why the government took so long? Your guess is as good as mine! We can say, we were the very first 'Family' Coast Guard personnel to be stationed there, but that is of little help. I just wanted to live there forever. STILL DO!!

Life goes on, and this story better be gittin' even though I would like to stay and dream of my Favorite Place!

When Ernie's military papers (his orders for transfer) arrived, I imagine I howled like a banshee. After being thrown together for the past three years, well thirty four months actually; we were to be separated. Ernie's orders were for a 'stag' (men only), semi-isolated station at Heron Neck L/S on Green Island, south of Vinalhaven Island, Maine.

"And what happens to Tommy, Lisa and me?" I wailed! Never made life easy for Ernie, did I? But, I did pick up and keep going - whenever and wherever! I'm looking for a pat on the back, I guess. On second thought, you'd better hold off for a spell and see if I deserve it.

Ernie found us a place to live. We called it the "Captain's House" even though it was owned by Colonel Johnson, in the town of Stockton Springs. It was his old home, and we rented just the down stairs of his huge house. There wasn't anything warm, soft or cozy here. Stark cold, reality and lonesomeness abounded. I just had to get hold of myself and make do for five year old Tommy and Little Lisa, who was almost three.

We were two 'glued' people, Ernie and I. He wasn't very happy about this latest assignment either. He had to do most of the cooking, along with his other duties, plus, the officer in charge was very difficult to get along with, plus - Ernie missed his family, plus, plus!

I was miserable, stuck at home all the time. I didn't drive then and I can't even remember how I got our food. Thank heavens for my folks who came at Thanksgiving and Christmas and brought us to their home for the holidays. Poor Ernie moped through them, alone part of the time on his 'deserted' isle.

To add to our bleakness, Ernie's Dad passed away, the 15th of December 1959.

There was an ironic twist to that story, too. Ernie called me the night of the 14th and demanded that I go to Waterville, the next morning. For me to call his sister, Freda, in Ellsworth; and see that we got there early. Alfreda got a baby sitter for her children (Philip aged 9 and Anna, age 8); knowing she wouldn't be there when they got home from school.

Freda arrived the next morning, early. We were all ready. Stopped in Belfast, at my folks, to leave Tommy and Lisa there, then flew as fast as the old VW bug would go.

As we entered sister Bernadette's drive, there were many cars already parked. Freda ran into the house. I took my time, gathering strength along the way. As I entered the kitchen, I noticed a black hat and coat and knew they must belong to a priest. I could hear soft voices saying prayers in the other room.

Dad, Joseph Edward DeRaps, looked so peaceful lying there on a stark white sheet, covered with a pretty blue blanket. With some of his loved ones circling his bed, Dad made a soft sigh, and was gone. To be with his lovely Maude, who had left him almost fifteen years before, in 1945. May GOD Bless you, Dad! I loved you as my own.

Ernie's premonition paid off, and I was glad to have made it to Waterville, in time to tell Dad we loved him and to go in peace. He had suffered long enough and had lived his 79 years well, though his last fifteen were lonesome for him. It was time to go HOME!

The second worse time of that day, was when I had to call Ernie with the news. There is no easy way to tell someone their loved one has died! I imagine when he heard my thick voice, he could tell, without being told - his Dad had passed away.

After Ernie returned to Heron Neck L/S from his emergency leave we missed each other even more and decided something had to be done about this separation.. We were sick and tired of not seeing each other, except every other month or so. We couldn't afford for him to fly into Belfast, unless it was an emergency, and by the time he took the ferry back and forth, there went two days of his leave. He started to look in 'earnest' for a rent on Vinalhaven Island. At least every time he came to the island for mail or food he could get to see his family for a few minutes, for hugs and kisses. We also knew, 'I was pregnant' with a baby due sometime in June. If we were going to move, lets do it before then.

The 29th day of February, 1960. Leap year, Yep! We leaped right across the water, from Stockton Springs to Vinalhaven Island, Maine (our sixteenth move since marrying. Actually, we had to gather up ALL of our junk, box it, put it in a truck, drive to Rockland, board a ferry for a long hour and a half ride.

Here we go again, FERRY RIDES. Only thing different, going to Vinalhaven, the trip was longer than to Monhegan. The island was much larger than Monhegan, it had more people, stores and a Main Street. But, this move would bring my family nearer to their "Daddy." That was why the move. Don't forget it, Polly! Just keep saying; Nearer, Nearer to your husband and the father of your children.

When I took one look at the place we would live in; there are words I could type, but I won't. Of all the weather-beaten, out of the way, god-forsaken looking areas. Yikes!!! And, to think I had to live here alone with the kids, hubby visiting only when he could.

Whether Thou goest, I go? Did I say that?? OH WELL, there was cold running water and three little cupboards in the kitchen. I won't go on! Let it be stated, I NO like!!

After 16 moves, I guess I could make some sort of a home out of this chaos, this eyesore. Home is home, no matter how homely! Tommy and Lisa loved the corner double lot. At least they had room to run and play, and the way the house was situated, I didn't have to worry about vehicles, because they belonged to our neighbors.

The neighbors! Now, there lies the best the island had to offer. Bud and Mary; June and Ben; Roz and Carl; Pat and Minzy; Francis, Harold and Frank; the Robertsons, Andersons, and Shields are just some of the names that come to mind even more than thirty years later.

Never shall I forget the good doctor Earle and his lovely mother, nor shall we forget the delicious meal we were served one night at their home. Never, never should I tell about the night I walked past their home. Doc had his bedroom window open and I whistled and shouted for him to get out of the window and stop showing off his polka-dot shorts! He could have crowned me for that comment! (What a terrible wit I have!)

Doctor Ralph Earle was one of the most intelligent men I have ever had the pleasure to meet. We struck it off immediately, and could have a conversation any time, day or night. If I had questions of any kind, just ask. He had started a clinic on the island that was tops in the nation, I do believe. Doc kept records of everyone and everything. It should have been the healthiest place to live in the state. He certainly worked hard enough to see to it. Plus, he was adored and admired by all who knew him. (I'd better write: "To the best of my knowledge!") Just because I loved him, doesn't mean everyone else did. He did have a gruff way about him at times, but he certainly knew medicine and preventative care. We had many talks about the latter. He thought I was trying to clean up the neighborhood, so gave me an A plus.

When some of the nicest or craziest things happened, you could bet Bud or Mary had something to do with it. They were good for a laugh, at least once a day or evening.

One of the nice times was exactly one month after we had moved to Vinalhaven. On the morning of the 29th of March, Mary showed up at my doorstep with the news that she had gotten me a baby-sitter for that evening, as she wanted me to visit her mother, Frances, with her.

I had met the intended sitter, knew Mary's mom didn't live very far, so if anything happened, I could be home in a shake, I said all right, I would go with her.

It was a nice evening as we strolled around the corner, gabbing away like magpies. Frances met us at the door, and, not being a nosy, gawking person, I looked straight ahead into the living room, where many people were gathered. I thought it might be a Tupperware or Make-up party, or something on that line. After a while, Mary said, "Let's go into the dining room for dessert."

I had wanted to finish my conversation with a lovely lady, so was almost the last one for eats. You will never know how dumb-struck I was when I heard, "Congratulations, Polly, on the coming birth of your baby." My GAWD, it was a baby shower for me. That darn Mary had gotten most of the neighborhood to come meet me and have a party. I didn't have the slightest idea, of course, but what they all giggled about was, when I came into the house, I had walked right by all the baby presents and decorations and never noticed them. I stated that I don't enter places, specially homes and notice things. I'm always interested in the people.

The party was wonderful, the desserts delicious and the gifts many and lovely. And needed! As Lisa was over three, her baby clothes had been given away a long time ago. Plus, I had not planned to have any more children. Tee Hee!

You see, I thought we three Fitzgerald sisters had made a pact to have our families before we were thirty. I was six and eight years older than them, so thought I did well when I had my first child at 26 and the second at 29, just under the wire. Joan was 21 and 23 when she had her daughter Marie and son Thomas. Anita was 21 when she had her first born Stephen, and was expecting in July 1960 when she would be 23. They married a lot younger than I did.

After the first week of June, I arrived to wait-out, at my folks' home. Instead, I spent a delightful week with my sister, Anita, her hubby Dean and almost two year old son Steven, who at the time lived in Brooks, Maine. Even though Anita was eight months along, they put much effort in re-doing a room just for my visit. With neither of us having a lap, little Steve had to have tea parties and stories read while we sat beside him. It was a fun, relaxing week and most appreciated.

I don't believe I had been back to my folks home more than a day or two, before Mother Nature decided it was time for some fireworks. I woke up Monday morning, June 20th. feeling very uncomfortable. Lower back pain and a big case of the blahs, that a hot cup of coffee or tea couldn't help.

I called Doctor Albro and gave him my symptoms. I wanted to know that he would be near when I needed him, more than anything.

Late afternoon I decided I'd had enough, so called Doc again, who told me to get myself down to the hospital. That made my parents extremely relieved. Guess they thought I was going to stay until the last minute. Daddy grabbed my suitcase and hardly gave me a chance to kiss Mom, before we were off.

Doc ushered me right into the labor room, as soon as I came in the door. He said I would have to wait for my supper, we had business to attend to.

At 6:29, on a beautiful evening the 20th of June, 1960; I was looking at the cutest bundle of love you ever saw. Six pounds, seven ounces and 19 1/2 inches long. Dark brown hair and big brown eyes, everything was perfect, except we didn't have a name. I was so sure the baby would be a boy, named Gregory Peter, I was at a loss for a girl's name. Every name I liked, Ernie didn't and vise versa. It's a wonder she didn't grow up being called Baby Girl DeRaps. We finally settled on Patricia in honor of Ernie's niece who was in a convent and had given up her birth-name, for Sister Wilfred. The name Mary was for her mother. Our little daughter Patricia Mary DeRaps was called Patty-cake for a long time, as that was her favorite game. Today she prefers to be called Patti.

A month to the day later, my sister Anita, had a boy and they named him Gregory Merle. Well, there goes that name; for me to use. There was a lot of talk when Joan named her son Thomas, after we had named our son that, in honor of our Dad. In the future, we tried to be more careful with names.

When Patti was just a few days old, I returned to Vinalhaven. With a wonderful doctor residing there, I had no qualms about going back early. Even Mother Nature cooperated, giving us a smooth ferry ride.

The DeRaps abode at Ingerson Street looked good to me, even though we had improvements to do. Moving to a new place, trying to get settled and having a baby, seemed to be all I could handle the past three months. Now that I was back, and the weather warmer, watch out dust and see me fly.

Summer time, windows open, two kids and a baby on a schedule, I could accomplish a great amount of work, in one day, trying to set the house in order. Ask neighbor, Mary. She used to walk in about ten A.M. and want to sit, talk and drink coffee. I might sit for a few minutes, but got up and worked around her. Most generally, she took the hint, and stayed just a short time; laughing all the way across the drive about how I loved to clean house. After a while, my keeping a clean home even rubbed off on her and we all were very proud of Mary's accomplishments.

That summer and fall, every spare minute Ernie had at home, we spent in making a foundation for a furnace, putting baseboard heaters in every room, plus installing all the pipes, tubes, fins, and anything else that goes into giving us oil fired baseboard heat for Maine's balmy winter days. We finished just about in time. In fact there was a nip in the air, when the new furnace blasted off for the first time. It was a good thing there was a stove for back up, that tells you how late in the season that we finished. Ah! What a wonderful feeling to be warm. Ernie did a good job as everything worked perfectly.

With our future so unsettled, I can't for the life of me figure out why Ernie bought this house, on the island. In the first place, why didn't he get a rent? Was he so desperate for us to be nearer, it was the only thing to do? Maybe there were no places to rent. Anyway, I certainly didn't want to spend the rest of my life on this island. And, owning a house that needed so much work wasn't feasible for us. Oh well, he bought the house and I made a home out of it, at least while we lived there. So what else is new? I'd done it before and I would do it again. Though, at the time, I thought only one more time.

Getting back to the cosmetic surgery needed for our Vinalhaven home. Much needed cupboards were never built, but he did make half of a hutch that I used for canned goods and pots and pans. It was a help.

The upstairs was a mess, so we used just the downstairs for quite a while. Bunk-beds were put in the front room, for Tommy and Lisa. Their bedroom should have been the living room. The dining room just held stuff and we never ate a meal there. The bathroom we fixed. Another tiny room with a full size bed shoved to a wall, plus Patti's crib, filled the room where I slept. We lived, ate and entertained in the kitchen. That room wasn't very large, either. A long hall, off the kitchen, held the freezer, boots, coats and culch. That was the down-stairs.

Upstairs were three rooms and a flush. They needed cleaning, painting and wall paper. The large room, over the kitchen, we did fix for a bed room for us. Ernie raised the roof and installed a large Anderson window that was lovely. It made the room airy and bright.

With time so precious, and little of it to accomplish anything, I am surprised we finished as much as we did. The house never received paint on the outside, nor did the double lot get manicured or flowers planted.

From October 1959 until July 1961, almost two years, Ernie spent on Heron Neck Light Station, while I grappled with every day living at the Vinalhaven house.

When Patti was three months old, Tommy started Kindergarten. That put us on a schedule, not that we weren't on one already. Washing, ironing, cleaning, nursing the baby, getting meals and snacks, tending to the neighbors problems and kids, it seemed the days were never long enough to do everything.

About this time, I was experiencing the pain and agony of having bursitis in my shoulders. Horrendous attacks would take me by surprise, every now and then. I had never before had anything like the pain I was having, but have lived with it all these years since, though not so bad. Accidents would happen too. Like the time I was carrying a teakettle full of boiling water to the table, my arm felt like it was dropping off and would sag, causing me to drop the kettle, hot water going everywhere, mostly on me. Picking up a plate of food, my arm would droop, loosing all muscle, food would go flying. The worse scenario was one time, with a baby in my arms. I had the presence of mind to stick my leg out and the baby slid down my leg right to the floor. Scared to pieces, but unhurt. That was when I called the doctor and said something had to be done right away, to ease the pain and help me over this new obstacle in my life. I was living on nerves, coffee and Darvon (doctor prescribed) nothing was helping. There had to be something out there to ease the pain I was having. And, I can stand more than most.

About this time, I decided to learn to drive a car. I was sick and tired of relying on Ernie or the neighbors. Being the independent witch, that I am, I wanted to get the mail or food, or take the children to the well baby clinic, or what ever, without bothering someone.

We had a pretty cream and green 1954 Chevy Bel Air, just sitting at the dock, waiting for Ernie to come to the island, and drive up to the house. There were plenty back roads to practice on. I don't remember getting us in too much trouble.

The day arrived to take my drivers examination. I was scared that I wouldn't pass, but I did it, with flying colors. I was asked a few questions, then told to start driving. We traveled a large square, and returned to the station, where he passed me a piece of paper. That's all folks. When I hear of all the trouble kids have today trying to get a license, I really giggle when I think of how I got mine. Although I don't care about driving and leave it to Ernie, I can do it if I have to. That's all that counts, as far as I'm concerned.

Now back to the last story I will tell about my bursitis. Doc Earle made me come right down to the clinic, the minute I could get a sitter for the children. Just by the tone of his voice I knew he was mad that I had put off getting the help he said he had.

I had hardly entered the door, when he hauled me into his office. After lambasting me out for not talking to him sooner, he came at me with a four inch long needle and said, "Polly, this is going to take effect in about four hours. It's going to hurt like hell, and you are going to call me every dirty name in the book, but, later you will feel better for it. I'm going to give you a cortisone shot. Sit down!"

I sat. I got the shot. I fainted. The first time ever. I sat up, slowly. I wiggled off the table. I fainted again. Finally, I said I was O.K., that I had to get home to the children and give them an early supper, before the shot took effect.

Once outside, I thought I would be fine, breathing the fresh air. I had just sat down behind the steering wheel, when, plop, over I went. By this time, I was madder than hell, wanting to know why I was fainting, and why did I bother having the shot if this was what was going to take place.

My cussedness, got me home, only to stop the car, a foot from the house. That was a close call. I fainted for the last time. Have never done it again. Never had another cortisone shot, either. That stinker didn't agree with me, wouldn't you say??

Then, like an idiot, I went up the hill for the children, instead of calling them home. Roz took one look at me, and ordered me to sit down. She had never seen anyone so white complected. She was scared for me, but, didn't say anything, when I started for home. Along the way, I hollered for Mary to bring Patti home to me.

The poor little kids got their supper and into their PJ's extremely early. I wanted to be ready for the assault the shot was to give me. Sure enough, it didn't take long before the pain was excruciating. Hours later, all alone and cried out, and yes I did call Doc every name in the book, plus some we had never heard of. I got up, made a cup of hot tea and warmed a bottle for Patti, as I had stopped nursing her.

As for the shot, it wasn't worth a tinkers damn, as far as I was concerned. I went right on having pain. Got sorta used to it after a few years. No pain killer worked for me, so stopped taking everything. Period! End of story!!

Heron Neck L/S duty, as I saw it:

Heron Neck Light Station (L/S) was situated on an eight acre island, called Green Island. Look on a map, and it's south of Vinalhaven. There was a light tower built in 1854 of brick and steel. A two story wood frame dwelling, 29 feet by 30 feet and a boat house 12 by 20 feet, built in 1899. An oil house of field stone was built in 1902. There was also a building to house the two gasoline powered electric generators but we don't have a record of when it was constructed.

The light was 92 feet above water and could be seen 14 miles away. Three men manned the station. No girls allowed, but, I got out there one day, thanks to Ernie.

It was Easter and he was all alone at the lighthouse. Unbeknown to me, Ernie had asked one of the local fisherman to bring me out to him that Easter. Of course he had gotten a sitter for our children, beforehand.

I remember two things about the day. The wonderful meal Ernie had prepared; ham, mashed potatoes, veggies, even apple pie and ice cream. Don't forget the biscuits, they were light and fluffy. His pie was better than mine!

I couldn't stay very long as the seas whipped up their "delightful ways" by 3 P.M. By the time I returned to Vinalhaven, I was soaked to the skin. Great for your complexion, but a terror for Bursitis. Nice cold, clammy, icy waters of Outer Penobscot Bay. (After a hot bath, I was none the worse for wear!) It was wonderful to see Ernie for three hours, taste his delicious cooking and visit where he lived and worked.

On a Sunday in August 1960, I almost became a widow, with three small children to care for!

On Heron Neck L/S, Sundays were most generally a day of rest, but you never knew when someone would be banging on your door for assistance. And, bang they did! That Sunday. A man, who looked like a drowned corpse, and two children - a little five year old girl and a boy of seven, came for help. They all were soaking wet, shivering from the cold water as well as scared to death.

The story came tumbling out of the man and boy. Their inboard motorboat had capsized in green water and giant waves. When the boat turned over, the tiny girl was trapped underneath. The man dove and was able to free her. He then righted the boat and got the two children into it. Finally, pushing the boat to a tiny beach. With his strength waning, he pulled, pushed and carried the children to the door of the light station.

They were going to be all right, but, there was another in the boat when it capsized, who managed to climb on to a surf-washed rock. He was an 18 year old boy from Massachusetts who couldn't swim and was waiting to be rescued!

A newspaper clipping stated: "Four survive when boat capsizes in rough water." That was correct, but the last typed words were, "Engineman Ernest DeRaps launched a motor skiff and pulled the tiring boy off." Ha, just like that, did he? Sounds so simple, so easy. Just putt-putt out, tell the lad to jump in, and putt-putt back whence he came. Not this time!

The waters of Hurricane Sound, off Green Island, can be and most of the time are; rough, green and hellish. Certainly no place to be with a tiny boat. That was beside the point. Some way, some how that lad had to be saved.

Ernie launched his own skiff, a 10 foot flat bottom, open boat with a 10 horse power motor, it being the only boat available as the station boat was off-island for repairs!

After making sure of the location of the boy, Ernie didn't have too much trouble in finding him. It was getting him off the rock, that was the problem. The young man was shivering from the ice cold water, shock and was petrified. He was afraid if he moved he would drown. (If he didn't, he would drown as the tide water would soon cover the rock.) Visualize his state, and along comes help, but the boy is too scared to help himself. Ernie had all he could do to keep the boat from filling up with water in the surf and keeping it from smashing on the rock.

"Timing is the most important thing," Ernie hollered to the boy. "When you see the bow come close to you, jump." Ernie might as well have been talking to the granite rock, for all the good it did. The lad was just too terrified to move.

Minutes turned into what seemed like an hour of pleading, the boat taking on water in the surf, hitting the rock several times as the seas surged. The waves were getting larger and the rock seemingly smaller as the tide rose. Both man and boy were getting extremely tired. If they didn't act soon, something drastic would happen, Ernie was positive of that.

Ernie backed off and came to the rock from another direction. As the small boat sided up to the rock, Ernie made a lunge for the boy and literally dragged him into the boat, almost capsizing on the spot. After catching his breath, Ernie steered through the heavy surf to the beach, grounded the boat, got the young man out and the two walked through the woods to the L/S.

Ernie prayed there would not be a repeat of this episode. In the next eleven months he would be stationed there, his prayers were answered.

A postscript to Heron Neck L/S . . . .

Since 1982, when the light was automated, the station was vacant and boarded up

BUT,

Sometime in the night, on the 28th of April, 1989; a fire broke out and severely damaged the light-house keepers home. The fire marshal thought this . . . "The station is powered by an underwater cable from Vinalhaven. A planned outage to allow the power company to repair the line was in effect. When the power was restored, a surge may have started the smoldering process. Faulty ceiling wire in the kitchen and bath area caused the fire that damaged the 135 year old building. No human element involved."

I should have learned to drive a car sooner than I did, because then the car would have been in our driveway, instead of where we found it.

There were many times while Ernie was stationed at Heron Neck, that he had a chance to motor-boat to Vinalhaven for mail and supplies. We thought leaving the car at the ferry boat terminal a great idea. Nobody would bother it. When Ernie came to town he could jump into the car, rush to the house to see us for a few minutes, tear off to do his errands, park the car at the terminal, hop into the boat and return to his island Station.

In the late 1800s Vinalhaven was noted for its granite quarrying. Beautiful granite columns still stand in many massive buildings around the United States, coming from Vinalhaven . . . and many broken, unfinished ones still dot the country side and off the roads of Vinalhaven.

One afternoon, there came a loud knock at my door. Bud, my neighbor said, "I guess you better come with me!" His wife Mary stayed to care for my imps. Figuring Bud was up to some foolish-ness, I left with him. I needed a break and he was always good for a laugh.

Bud didn't drive more than three miles from the house. We stopped on a road I was familiar with because of a 60 foot long piece of intriguing looking granite near the road. Only thing wrong this day, I wasn't interested in seeing the massive block of granite; I wanted to know who's car had hit it and was lying smashed up and on its roof.

A loud cry of anguish came out of my mouth, "My God, that's my car." "What in hell, is it doing over here?" I screamed. I was so distraught, Bud almost backhanded me before I could calm down and make sense. I was told that sometime during the night two local troublemakers - young hooli-gans - fixed the wires and went for a joy ride. Only thing, they didn't know how to drive, pushed the accelerator to the floor; tires caught in the sand and flipped the car onto its back but not before hit-ting the huge hunk of granite and landing beside my favorite column. The joy-riders had to break out the rear window before they could crawl out of the car, as the doors were jammed shut. Neither of the two boys were hurt.

Not hurt, eh? Smart asses, you say? Let me get hold of them for a few minutes and we'll see about that. I'll take a two by four to their butts, then you'll see smart asses. They won't be able to sit for a week.

You are not supposed to say you love a material object. Bull!! I loved our 1954 Chevy Bel Air - cream and a pretty green in color and best of all, it was all paid for. Damn it! What do we do now? Someone found us a used car, a piece of junk, but that's another story.

Capers on Vinalhaven

All work and no play, make Jack a dull boy!

You have to be a little crazy to get along in this world.

Most of the time, I am a serious wife and mother. I don't tolerate much foolishness from the children or anyone else, for that matter. Don't ask me why. I suppose because there wasn't much fun around when I was growing up. Everyone worked so hard to make a living, there wasn't time to act silly. Actually, I can't think of one comic in the whole family.

My seriousness didn't stop a few people on the island, from coming to our home and having fun.

How about the morning in dead winter, when looking out the window, all I could see was snow piled up about six feet beside the porch.

It had been a brute of a snow storm on the island. I didn't have the foggiest idea where the wind would pile the snow in drifts. Knowing I had to keep a path open to the back door, I went and dressed in my heaviest clothing, boots and mittens.

I had just opened the kitchen window, to crawl out with shovel in hand, when the door opened and there stood Bud, explaining what a mighty storm we'd had during the night, and where the hell did I think I was going, and why - out the window? That cussed, wonderful neighbor, had gotten up at the crack of dawn and shoveled me out, knowing my husband wasn't at home and Bud didn't want me to do it.

Boy! Didn't he tease me about trying to crawl out the window. Didn't he laugh when I told him about the high mound of snow beside the window which I thought Mother Nature had brought to my door. Bud had purposely shoveled it high, just so I would think what I did.

How about the time, when I was cleaning house and not paying any attention to Mary who was playing with our daughter Patti, on her first birthday. Unbeknown to me, Mary was giving her a chocolate candy bar, while Patti was sitting in her new WHITE highchair.

They were laughing and having so much fun . . . until I turned around to see what was so funny. I let out a holler so loud that Patti started crying, but, Mary laughed so hard she looked like she was crying too.

I had never seen such a mess. Chocolate was spread all over the highchair and my child looked like a brown bear. When Mary recovered, she said, "It was worth your ire, you clean, neat person, you. I have wanted to do something like that, ever since I met you, Polly!" And with that, Mary proceeded to clean up the mess, she loved to see happen. I guess that put me in my place for constantly keeping a clean home. We sat down, had a cup of coffee and laughed over my foolishness.

Even at this late date, I have to giggle over the antics of Frank and Walter. Those two 'nuts' were forever thinking up crazy doings.

One evening, those two arrived, walked into my kitchen, crying and carrying a big pail of water. I couldn't imagine what they were crying for. They told me to look in the pail. I did, and saw seven tiny fish. The boys said they were dying. Couldn't I do something about it?

Yes, I sure could. For starts, I passed them the mop and told them to clean up the water they were spilling all over the floor. Then, I took a bottle of wine, poured some in the pail, and made the sign of the cross. The fish wiggled, the boys giggled and returned home, laughing all the way down the street.

While stationed at Brown's Head L/S, the boys telephoned us one night, about nine o'clock, and said they wanted to visit and asked if I could make some brownies for them. I made the brownies, two pans in fact, and sat them over in a corner to cool.

The boys arrived, we talked for quite a while, then they asked if I had cooked something for them. I went to the kitchen, made coffee, turned to get the brownies, only there were none to be seen.

Oh, oh. The boys were up to their old tricks again. Sure enough, out they came, asking for their dessert. "You find them," I said. "I know you've hidden the brownies some place."

To placate them, I opened all the cupboard doors. "See," I said. "No brownies here." I opened the refrigerator door, even the oven door. All the time, those two screwballs were laughing their heads off. Finally, I sat down. "That's it, no more looking."

Where did they hide the brownies? In the clothes dryer. Wouldn't that have been a nice mess, if I had added wet clothes, without looking inside first. That would have given them something to hoot about, if they had heard, wouldn't it? Yes indeed!

Nice quiet evenings were had, whenever Bud's mother visited the island. There wasn't anything better than Amelia and me and a spot of tea, at midnight. We relaxed, talked softly, or said nothing. Just sitting there listening to the nighttime sounds was so peaceful. More than one night was spent like that. We have beautiful memories. She lived in Rockland, and was 93 in August of 1994.

I guess you might say, there are times when I don't pay attention to what I'm saying or doing. I really pulled a "boner" the day I met Pat a young wife and mother who had just moved into a house behind ours. It was early spring and I was outback trying to clean up our yard, when I came across a pair of men's briefs. Yes, you've already guessed it. When the young woman came outside, I asked if they belonged to her husband, while I waved the dirty piece of clothing in the air. Isn't that the dumbest thing you ever heard of?

She had the greatest sense of humor I have ever seen in anyone. And, it was a good thing for me that she did.

"Hell no, they don't belong to him. Sure they don't belong to yours?"

Then I put my foot in my mouth by saying, "He doesn't live here with me." I was just getting in deeper and deeper, so shut up for a minute, then introduced myself as that dumb bunny Polly who is your neighbor.

She laughed, a hearty sound came from her, then she said, "I'm Pat, come over and have a cup of coffee, while I wait for the kids to come home from school."

Even with my faux pas, we became the greatest of friends. When Ernie came in, many evenings were spent at one house or the other, playing Password. Girls against the boys, of course. We played dirty too. But the night we girls came up with the word "bullgirl" for "cowboy," the men thought we had gone too far. They were furious, while we roared with laughter, thinking how smart we were to come up with the magic word for us to win. Oh, the tricks we pulled, playing that game.

I had never met a person who had more vim and vigor than Pat. She had enough energy for ten women, with some left over. I do believe, she up and went, before she started. She was bold and brazen. No one could top her in anything, be it work fast, laugh the loudest, fly up the island in her convertible, with her hair blowing in the sonic speed she so loved, the fastest dance, Pat was just a speed demon in everything.

I don't remember which one of us moved first, I mean off the island. I think she did, and no doubt it was a good thing. For me, that is. If I had stayed around her very long, I'm afraid I would have picked up some of her bad habits. Any gullible person was in for trouble, if they hung around Pat very long, believe me. You would just get caught up in her antics, her speed, her zest for life. She was exhausting to be with. But, how we loved her. The last I heard, she was living in St. George. Poor town, never knew what hit them when she arrived. Maybe she is the town manager today. Wouldn't surprise me, any. Beautiful, bold, brazen, bubbly, batty, Patty. No, just call me Pat, she would say. Whatever word you choose, you'll get love in return. Love you kiddo, wherever you are.

That word was in the wind again, TRANSFER. We found out it would be the easiest move we ever had. We would leave our home for Browns Head Lighthouse, which was about 7 miles away. We didn't even have to leave the island. Just gather our clothes, our food and move - up island.

After almost two years, we would become a family again. Ah! To have a man around the house sounded delicious. Just maybe Ernie could take some of the load off my shoulders for a while. I certainly felt like I needed someone to talk, discuss, even argue with, besides the children. Most of the time telephones make for yearnings, and most definitely miserable bedmates. Not that I needed one at the time, you understand. I was seven or eight months pregnant with child number four. Right then, all I wanted was a back warmer and someone to talk with. Guess who? My husband!

Brown's Head L/S

Brown's Head Light Station is on the northwest side of Vinalhaven Island, the West entrance to Fox Islands Thorofare. A white cylindrical tower rises 39 feet above the water. The white sector is 3,000 candle power, the red sectors are 600 candle power and the light is visible for 11 miles. This station was built in 1832 and was bolted to the side of a cliff a short distance above the high tide mark. The tower is connected to a wooden white dwelling. A boathouse was slightly below and north of the dwelling. A fog signal bell tower was also North of the dwelling. Reached by walking along a plank deck and about 50 feet away.

The first of July 1961, we became the 10th Keeper of the Light at Brown's Head. Our stay would be only 16 months. The U.S. Coast Guard likes to keep you moving. Some different than the olden days, when you were Keeper for decades or until you died.

I had hardly unpacked and got things organized before it was time to cross the bay, for a stay with my folks pending the birth of our next child. I never heard what an imposition it was for Ernie's sister, Bernadette, who arrived to stay with him and the children.

Ernie brought me to Belfast, the 2nd of August, he stayed overnight then returned to the island the next day. A relief keeper, came and tended to business in Ernie's absence; that's a C.G. MUST.

Tommy was a big help for his Auntie. He was almost seven, going on seventeen? Lisa was 4 1/2 and at an age where she could do for herself, thank you! Fourteen month old Patti was the one who needed assistance. Just keeping her out of mischief was a full time job. Summertime when the living was easy. No schedules to follow, made lighter work for Bunny (Bernadette).

It was good to see the folks again, as it had been a long time between visits. Plus, I needed a rest very much. I was really stretched out from moving, bursitis attacks and this pregnancy was too soon after the last one. We all are entitled to one goof, right? I just think my hormones went into overdrive, that's all.

Dad was noted for getting up early and making coffee. The aroma drifted into the bedroom, that beautiful summer morning, the 9th of August 1961. I had been only half sleeping, so got up and joined Dad for a cup of his strong brew.

About an hour later, I asked if he had plans for the day, that I might need him to drive me to the hospital, before the day was over. I was starting to feel very uncomfortable. That made him grab another cup of java for himself, and got one for Mom, who was still asleep.

I just happened to think about this, this was the third pregnancy I had burdened the folks with. Shame on me, but, I can't think of a better place to be or people to be with. Thank God they were there, for I didn't want to have my babies at home on the island. NO way!

It just so happened I had a doctor's appointment at noon that day with dear old Dr. Albro. I wondered if I would make it until then.

Dad drove me down to the office. I told him to wait, for I was sure I wouldn't be very long.

The minute Doc saw me, he yelled, "What in hell are you doing back here so soon?" He knew Ernie was on a stag station, Heron Neck Light, and I lived at our home on Vinalhaven. Real serious, I said, "I must have caught a germ, over the telephone." With a disgusted look on his face, Doc grabbed me by the wrist and pulled me into the examination room.

It only took a minute to see that I was about ready to produce something. Doc said, "Do you have your suitcase with you, if not, go get it and I'll meet you at the Waldo County General Hospital in 20 minutes."

When I returned to the car, I gently told Dad what Dr. Albro had said. He put his foot to the pedal. Full speed home. I kissed Mom, Dad grabbed my suitcase and varzoom, down the avenue we went, taking the hospital driveway on two wheels.

As we entered the door, Doc was waiting for me. I kissed Dad and told him to go home and keep the speedometer under forty.

Doc must have had plans for the rest of the day, because he gave me a shot of some kind and the labor pains immediately became violent. I went through the three stages of birth in just over and hour, and believe me, I would not recommend that to anyone.

At 2:28 P.M. on 9 August 1961, I delivered a tiny 6 pound 4 ounce, 19 1/2 inch long son. He would be known as Peter Gregory DeRaps. A name we had previously chosen, but turned around; seeing my sister had named one of her sons Gregory. I was bound to get that name in there some how. It is Ernie's middle name, and the name Peter (which means "rock"), felt correct. After looking into my baby's brown eyes, I knew he would have a solid, stable affect on everyone he would meet.

That lovely Wednesday evening, at precisely 7 P.M., Mom and Dad entered my room, beaming. "My Gawd, if I'd known you were going to take such a short time, I'd hung around to see my latest grandson." Dad said, "I should know how fast you do things by now, though." I asked if they had already seen my new baby, but it was a foolish question. By the tears and bright smiles, I knew they had. "So," I asked. "What do you think about him? Is he a keeper?"

"Yep, that he is," Dad said smiling. "He's so tiny, I think I'll put him in my pocket and take him fishing."

I grieve to write about this next part of my life, but not having much time left before returning to the island and my family obligations, I had a mission to accomplish.

My Grampa Fenwick was very ill in the Bradbury Memorial Hospital. Unfortunately it had been ages since we last saw one another. Something told me to go see him before going home. The hospital wasn't far from my folks house, so after getting Peter settled in for a few hours, I informed the folks I was going to stroll over and see Grampa.

Dad wanted to take me in the car, but I told him the fresh air and exercise would be good for me.

Nothing or no one could have prepared me for the look of him. My dear, dear Gramps was so white as he lay there on that stark white sheet. His face was racked with pain, his long, gnarled fingers were opening and closing, as if he was trying to decide if he would fight or accept his situation. His beautiful blue eyes were closed, his mouth open and above that hole was the huge walrus mustache which he'd had since I could remember. Didn't I hate that darn thing. He was forever trying to get me to kiss him, knowing how I despised that mass of bristly hair.

That evening, when he finally woke up a bit, glory be, he recognized me. I bent over and kissed him right on his mouth. We hugged a lot but talked very little. Mostly we held hands

I had not been there very long, before Gramp's son Frederick arrived. Right off the bat, he wanted to know how I had gotten to the hospital. When I told him I had walked, he cussed me out first class.

I can hear his loud voice, even now, say, "Pauline, didn't you just have a baby, don't you know you should be resting. What are you doing up and around, anyway? You should be in bed!"

On and on my dear uncle ranted. I tried to tell him it was the 20th century. Women no longer stay in bed for weeks and lose their muscle, like his mother did. Today, we have a baby and get up a few hours later, providing there are no complications. He just could not accept the fact. Anyway, when it was time to leave, I let my uncle drive me back to my folks home. When we arrived, he started talking to my mother, his sister, all about my gallivanting. I almost got a stomach ache from laughing at him. Love you Unk. I do know you only had my welfare at heart.

Saturday morning, 19th August, dawned bright and beautiful. Peter was 10 days old. It was time to go home and introduce him to his father, brother Tommy and sisters Lisa and Patti. I was missing them all terribly, so it was me who was pushing to be off. Mom and Dad were having kittens to see me leave so soon. With the good doctor on the island, again I felt very safe in returning to Vinalhaven and getting reacquainted with our new abode, Brown's Head Light Station.

Dad drove us to the ferry terminal in Rockland and saw us safely seated on the ferry before he would leave. He promised that he and Mum would come out to visit us soon. The smell of the sea was making him hanker for some of those crawly things that turn red when cooked. Lobsters I'm talking about, in case you don't know.

I had barely gotten settled in my seat on the ferry, when I was approached by a couple and asked if I was Polly DeRaps and if my baby was Peter Gregory. I had never seen these nice looking people before, maybe it was someone Ernie had met. Yes, I was right. The man said, "Let me introduce us. I am Tom Dozier and this is my wife Florence. We have just had the pleasure of meeting your husband and your lovely children, four days ago, when we walked to the lighthouse. We are renting a cottage not far from there, for the summer. We were so taken by your family, that when your husband stated you were coming home today, we offered to come over and escort you home, knowing he couldn't leave his duties."

There was something about those two, that put me at ease immediately. I even let Florence hold my baby for awhile, to rest my shoulders and answer her pleas to do so. Tom looked the tourist; wearing tan slacks, plaid shirt with the sleeves partly rolled up, a sweater tied around his waist and sneakers with nice thick soles. Good for walking. Florence reminded me of an Indian Princess. Dark complected, dark brown hair pulled back and plaited into one long braid. She wore a peasant blouse, long skirt and sandals. She had what I call an educated face, and well she should.

Tom worked for *Time-Life* magazine and they traveled all over the world, having just returned from Italy and England. The latter, Florence adored and could live there forever, not just the few short years they had.

This was the beginning of a beautiful friendship that has lasted over thirty years.

When the ferry docked at Vinalhaven, pandemonium broke out as my family all tried to reach us first. Hugs, kisses, squeals of "Let me see the baby." and "I want my Mama" coming from tiny, almost a baby herself, Patti. The nice couple I had just met were on the side line taking in all of our excitement, and lost in the shuffle for a while, but, to my delight, we all squeezed into the car and started for home.

Ernie dropped the Doziers off at the cottage, with the promise we would walk over to see them soon. and, if that wasn't soon enough, they could come see us any time.

It was soooo good to be home again, though I had forgotten we had to park the car at the top of the steep hill and walk down a long ramp to get to the house. With everyone pitching in, all supplies came down in one trip.

Dear sister Bernadette had supper all ready for us, and don't you think that wasn't a treat for me. Yes, indeed. After taking care of Peter and putting him to bed, my full time was spent listening to the children relate all that had happened while I was away for those seventeen days, which seemed like 17 years to them. Ernie too. All the time Tommy and Lisa were talking, Patti sat snuggling in my lap. She wasn't going to let anyone have her mother for sometime. Later, when I tucked her into her bed, she would holler, "Mama, you there?" This went on for hours.

Finally, with the two little ones sleeping, it was time to give Tommy and Lisa my undivided attention. When you are almost seven and four and a half, you need your mother for a while and to know she is going to stay and be there at home. After several times of going out to play and returning to see your mother is still there, you feel comfortable. Then after awhile, you almost forget she had left, and you return to your old ways of taking her for granted, as most children do.

It was late evening, after Peter had his bottle, around 11 P.M. before Daddy got the attention he needed. Poor Daddies, always last when there are little ones around. Oh well, put a stopper on it and just maybe you would have more time with "Mom."

Eighteen days after returning home, I received the news that my Grampa Fenwick had passed away. Free from pain at last, on this day; the 6th of September, 1961.

I knew what the news would be, the minute I heard my father's voice. I knew it would not be long, twenty days ago, when I walked over to the hospital to see Grampa. I knew it would be the last time I would see him. I knew when I kissed that beautiful mouth. I knew my dear Gramps would never recover and his passing was for the best. Of course, it didn't stop me from sitting down and crying my heart out.

My Gramps had lived 88 years. Well over half of those years, after a horrendous accident, he was stooped and favored one leg. Still it didn't stop him from carrying on farming, haying, cooking and caring for his children. He liked his tea black, his "tobaccie" strong and had a passion of looking at a woman's trim ankle. Of course when he married Grammie back in 1900, that was all a lady showed, until she took off her gloves.

Gramps was a kind gentle soul. To us grandchildren he was the best story teller, the best gingerbread cake maker, his vegetables were the biggest and his apple orchard grew the brightest, tastiest apples we ever ate.

My uncles, especially John and Bill Fitzgerald could never get enough of his strong tea and tall tales. All three have passed away since, but I suspect heaven hasn't been the same since they arrived. Deer stories, tea, gingerbread cake and plenty of laughter.

Gramp had a long, lean, lanky body. His sparkling blue eyes twinkled deviltry and he was always ready to hear a story, and sometimes, when the 'boys' got out of hand and told a raunchy one, Gramp would let out a raucous laugh, slap his knee and say, "Ain't that rich!"

His actions would set the 'boys' laughing so hard, they were almost crying. Holding onto their stomachs, they would reel outdoors to catch their breath, pee behind the barn, then return for more tea and stories. I never saw the antics, just heard about them, a million times at least.

Of course, Grammie was always in bed, when the jokes, stories or wild tales were told. She would have been mortified to death on hearing any of them. As it was, if Gramps told something just a tiny bit off color, she'd say, "Now Fred." That's all it took. He'd shut right up.

Dear Grampa, he didn't have much fun in his long life, so I guess if he got some enjoyment listening to two young fellows telling stories, good or bad, once a year in November at deer hunting time, I do believe, all is forgiven.

Gramps believed in the Lord and to prove my point - - - Late in life, he was getting very deaf and it bothered him terribly. Every Sunday morning, he listened to a preacher on his tiny television. One day the sermon was on healing. Gramp hobbled to the set, laid his hand on top of the TV and cried out, "Heal my ears so I might hear better."

Blessed Savior! Gramp could hear a normal sounding voice, the rest of his life. That is believing . . . . I loved you Grampa.

Having just given birth to my son and returning to the island , there was no possible way I could attend Gramps funeral in Morrill, Maine; at the church, across from the cemetery. I certainly was there in spirit. My memories of Grampa, Fred Fenwick, will live with me until I see him again.

As I recall, the rest of the year was uneventful. On the 11th of November Tommy celebrated his 7th birthday, having a group of school friends arrive for cake and ice cream.

A powerful rain storm did arrive in the fall, leaving my cleaned living room windows covered with salt spray. What a mess that was to clean up. As stated before, the house was bolted to the side of the cliff, so any strong storm could reach up about 15 feet to deposit salt spray on the windows. From inside, the storm looked mighty scary, especially to the children.

A steep 200 foot long walkway was fine from spring to fall but the winters were a different story. Not only was it hard to shovel, it was a stinker to climb.

One winter day, after a snowstorm, the wind was so fierce, Ernie tied a rope around Tommy's waist and hauled and slipped to the top, in order to reach the car; to take him to the school bus; which then took Tom to school. Tommy couldn't wait to tell his school friends about the storm, his mother hollering to be careful; while he was having so much fun and his Dad tying the rope around his waist.

Nothing could be finer than be given permission to catch a lobster or two, now and then. Ernie got his license and was allowed to set out four or five traps near the station. After a long days work, about 10:30 at night, when I had relaxed some, I'd say, "I'm hungry." Ernie always knew what was in store for him. So, I'd help him put the boat in the water; while he went out, I'd grab a pail of salt water, return to the house and start it to boil. Then return to the boathouse and help him winch the boat up the slip.

Just in time for the 11 o'clock news, we'd sit down to a feast fit for the gods. I can hear some people exclaim, "Not that time of night, for such rich food. You'll never sleep!" Ha! Want to bet? Just like a baby, I did. Ernie might have to take some Mallox, now and then, but that was the DeRaps stomach "talking."

Staying on the delicious subject of lobsters, I want to relate about someone else who could never get his fill of those creatures, my Dad.

On a delightful spring day in 1962, my folks kept their promise and came for a visit. We were prepared to feast my father all weekend, if need be. The night of their arrival, I think Dad ate four lobsters. I don't mean just the claws and tail, I mean the meat out of the legs and body also. It's a picking slow process job, but you never let a morsel go to waste. That is sinful. Next morning, for breakfast, it was lobster on toast. For lunch, lobster stew. And again, for supper; lobster. The next day, Daddy ate very lightly, only soups and sandwiches and such.

"By Gawd, for once in my life, I've had my fill of those red things," Dad said with a grin. "I never thought I'd say such a thing, but I am now. Thanks to Ernie's hard work and Polly's know how, thank you very much."

It was a delightful weekend which we've never forgotten. The four children were on their best behavior, though they kept their grandparents busy every minute. Showing them their rooms and toys, taking them up to the light; with their fathers assistance. Informed them how the bell in its tower worked. Walked them up the steep walkway, then on a nature trip. My folks certainly got the royal tour, and Tommy, Lisa and Patti never stopped talking all the while.

I enjoyed watching them all. My parents didn't get many chances to see the children so this made the weekend very special. Daddy even carried baby Peter on some of their excursions which was a surprise as he never cared to handle little children. Afraid he would drop them, I guess.

That summer was wonderful. The Doziers returned for a vacation; of course we saw a lot of each other. Hearing all about their past year and travels proved an education in itself. Tasty meals with them and talk over a nice glass of wine. Voila!

That whole summer was exciting with much company, many picnics, lobster feasts, fun and laughter. We had one full month of fog, with the bell clanging day and night. You do get used to it, though. After the third week, it would be nice to hear something else. Nice to see something too. Like the big boat pulling seven smaller craft and behind them an airplane on pontoons. We could just make them out in the fog.

At times, it was scary when you heard a noise on the water and couldn't see what it was. When you knew the ferry to North Haven or pleasure craft were in the vicinity, you knew the ferry would make their destination but the others were idiots, being out in that kind of weather and taking a chance to get to where they were going. Some people are so stupid. Not only are they risking lives, but they were driving me crazy with fear for them. I was not anxious to prove my worth trying to save their dumb hides. And I most certainly didn't want the father of my children to have to risk his life either.

We'd already had our share of excitement and confusion, which I will relate shortly.

That summer of '62, was a time when Ernie and I were the closest and most loving. We enjoyed being together, even though we were constantly together twenty four hours. We laughed together, we cried together. We paid more attention to the children. We just love life together. Wasn't it a wonderful thing, we didn't know that in four months our lives would be turned upside down and we would be separated. Maybe that is why that summer seemed so special, the Lord was telling us to grasp every minute and live life to the fullest.

That is why I started the last paragraphs, that summer, I wanted to remember the good times, the love we shared with each other as well as with the children. The lobster feasts, the picnic, the company. I even wanted to remember the long month of fog, the walks on the shore when the tide was out. The day I kicked into what I thought was a water soaked log, only to find out it was a sea cucumber about a foot long. Surprisingly, when I kicked it, it shrunk to about four inches. Yuck! What a homely looking thing. I had never seen that creature before, or since.

Back to the week of confusion. It may sound like our life was just steady days of fun and games, while living on the Lighthouse Station. Ah! How we wished. The government supplied the materials, but we had to produce the brains and brawn. Inspection time was coming soon. Three officers were arriving the first of October, from Boston, for the Eastern Area Inspection, which everyone dreaded. This was the BIG ONE! The inspection that could make or break you, swiftly and easily with just a signature.

Everything, and I do mean everything, had to look like it was brand new. Starting at the top of the hill, where we had a small area to park vehicles, down a long, boarded walkway; to the bell tower, walk a platform deck to the house, and / or, down a shorter walkway to the boat house and slip. The light tower was connected to the main house on the far side, where there was a small plot of lawn and the flagpole.

From the top of the hill down to the waters edge, was a considerable large area to keep cleaned, mowed, painted, washed, scrubbed, swept, polished; inside and outside of the bell tower, boathouse, light tower and the house we resided in with four small children.

For a few days we didn't take many coffee breaks, but, the answer is to be constantly prepared, then there isn't so much extra to do. Be prepared. Be ready, at ALL times!

My Coast Guard husband, our four children, and I were living at Brown's Head Light Station, off the coast of Maine, on Vinalhaven Island. We had put in a long laborious day of scraping paint off the deck from the dwelling to the bell tower. An area about 8 feet wide by 40 or so feet long. A protective fence between the buildings, on the shore side, had been painted white the day before. The deck would be painted battleship gray.

Finished for the day, we planned to have a cup of coffee out on the front porch and survey our surroundings. It was a lovely calm evening, we didn't get many of them as most generally there was a heavy evening breeze. The night was perfect to sit and hear the water slapping gently on the boat slip, to see the distant city lights of Rockland twinkle on and to watch the nearby bell-buoy gently rock to and fro in the middle of the Thorofare making a soft gong, bong sound. We listened to the birds saying good night to each other and thanked God for all our blessings, this soft, gentle evening.

The telephones loud ring jarred us out of complacency. The urgent request came over the wires, loud and clear. Had we heard any airplanes in the past half hour? Yes, we had. In what direction was it headed? East, about 15 minutes ago. The call, so they said, had come from a Coast Guard Base person. If so, he was definitely rattled. Maybe he was new in the service, because he was using gutter language, hollering we didn't know anything and he slammed down his receiver hard enough to break an ear drum.

This had never happened before, so we thought it must have been some idiot who was mad at the military.

Minutes later the phone rang again. This time the voice was more professional. He was from the Air Force, but he asked the same question as the first. And, he received the same answer.

Wondering what in the world was going on, we immediately turned the radio on to a Coast Guard frequency and heard that a "T-33" training jet had crashed in Penobscot Bay.

Reports on what happened differed greatly. People thought they heard a plane crash in widely scattered areas. Some declared they'd heard voices on land as well as in the water. Others were sure they had heard cries of pain or help in different sections.

Confusion reigned. Suddenly without warning all of our gentle feelings were forgotten, for death and destruction were at hand.

We did our small part by going up in the tower and on the hill behind the dwelling and scanned the bay with binoculars. There was not much day light left, but we stayed at our post for hours, with the exception of one of us going to listen to the radio, every 15 minutes.

On another island, a Coast Guardsman, believing he too had heard strange sounds, went to investigate, in his rowboat. After a trip around his island station, he headed out to sea. Just outside the harbor he thought he saw a faint light. Making a bee-line for it, he found a man. Hauling him into the small craft was no easy task, as the heavy wet clothing was cumbersome and the man was getting weaker.

In the distance we could see a buoy tender barreling their way to the rescued man. It wasn't long before they had him aboard and administering first-aid. He informed them, he was the pilot of the crashed jet, and asked if anyone had picked up his passenger.

On the radio, we heard the pilot, a Captain, state that they were returning to their base from Washington, D.C. His passenger was a Major, just out of the hospital and a friend. At the airfield the pilot had offered his friend a ride back to their base.

When the Captain was asked what happened, he said, "Just a few air miles short of our goal, flying at 15,000 feet, the generator failed. With no lights, no way to communicate, I informed the Major I would blow the canopy at 8,000 feet, and for him to eject at once. I would wait a few seconds and eject also. This I did, but, in the rush of wind and in the darkness, I couldn't tell if the Major bailed out or not. "On coming down, the first thing the Captain noticed were the lights of a town or city and secondly, he was going to land in the water, well off shore.

Where, was the Major?

The search grew more tense. By midnight, we could see that more planes, ships, and boats of all kinds had been pressed into service. All night long, they criss-crossed, north, south, east and west, maneuvering around small or large islands.

At 3:30 A.M. I had decided to rest a bit, when the whole thoroughfare lit up. I wasn't long in going downstairs to find my husband and the cause of such brightness. Inside the house was as bright as outside. I shuddered to think what had taken place. This was eerie, hauntingly so. What a relief to hear Ernie say that a Coast Guard plane from Rhode Island had just dropped flares over the bay, one almost in front of the house.

Later in the morning, I found my husband back up in the light tower, scanning the shore and water. The search had gone on all night and would continue until night fall, when they had to return to their bases for fuel and sleep.

I had slept from four 'til six, when I had to get Tommy off to school. Short night but I didn't think much about anything, except where was the Major. While Ernie drove Tom to the school bus, I scanned the waters all the while getting breakfast for our other three children. With Lisa's help they ate and got dressed. Forget housework this day.

The day proved fruitless, though there were times, our hearts would soar hoping and praying the latest clue would be the right one and they could end the search.

Radio reports of a parachute on a mountain top, turned out to be an old weather balloon. Cries or noises were animals or birds. What looked like something in a distance, a closer look would reveal a log or nothing of importance. Extensive searching narrowed to a harbor, not far from where the Captain was picked up.

For five days — five very long days, sonar and scuba divers worked diligently. For all their efforts they only found portions of a wing tip, a fuel tank and pieces of clothing. For all the heartbreaking labor that went on, day after weary day, they never found the Major or jet plane.

The seventh day was the most heartrending of all. Watching through binoculars, we could see the buoy tender riding at anchor near the harbor. On board were the Major's wife, children, family and friends. After a short memorial service, the widow tossed a wreath upon the water.

Existing on four or five hours sleep per night for almost a week; using binoculars until our eyes felt like they would pop out; constant scanning the water and shore; the radio blaring continuously; eating in snatches; on the run to do a child's bidding; all of this was slowly wearing us down. Actually, we were exhausted, but under the circumstances we would have gone on indefinitely if need be. That's what we were here for! That's what the United States Coast Guard stands for; helping, searching and rescuing.

We were so fatigued! About the same time the memorial wreath hit the sea, we slid down on our knees and said a prayer. Then, the tears flowed!

That evening, after attending to just what needed to be done, we, once again, were on the porch, sipping a cup of hot coffee. The light in the tower was shining brightly across quiet, calm waters. It was so tranquil. I couldn't help thinking about the widow and her small children. I prayed she would find the serenity that we beheld that night.

We took a few days to recuperate and spent precious time with our children, who by the way, had been a great help during our week of confusion. A short trip to the mainland before school vacation ended, really helped put our thoughts back into proper prospective.

We returned to the station, relaxed and ready to put the finishing touches to the upcoming Eastern Area Inspection. We were so sparkly clean, we squeaked. The small lawns were manicured from the top of the hill down and around the dwelling. Everything that needed painting was painted, the brasswork shown so bright you needed sunglasses to admire it, a clean curtain was placed over the light lens in the tower, a new United States flag slapped in the breeze. We were starched and pressed in new clothing, all six of us. I could not possibly see a mistake. We were as close to perfect as possible, I thought. Now, let us see what the great inspectors think.

Wednesday, the 3rd of October 1962; dawned bright and beautiful, I prayed the day would end the same.

At precisely 1 P.M., three inspectors arrive from the First Coast Guard District Headquarters of Boston, MA. The first thing I noticed was the stark white gloves. After being introduced, I was supposed to become invisible, I thought. Not this time. One man stayed with Ernie, one with me, and the third snooped, gawked, pried, opened and you name it. Shortly, they would swap places, until all three had talked individually with us and satisfied their curiosity.

One of the men looked like trouble to me. He was rough, gruff and had no personality. Wouldn't you know, HE was the one who said, "Meet me at your dining room table!" The minute he spoke, I froze. I knew we were in trouble, but for the life of me, I couldn't imagine why. We followed him into the house, where he proceeded to lay all kinds of papers over the table.

Sternly, he told us to sit down. I was so startled by his angry mood, I pulled out a chair, and not looking, sat smack down on his military dress hat, crushing the top. I didn't know he had left it there.

He started a lengthy tirade. His major comment was; why was it Ernie had never had sea duty after all the years he had been in the Coast Guard?

We never thought it a prerequisite to being a Coast Guardsman. After nearly seven years of service, we had never been approached about sea-duty. Why now? Why was this inspector so adamant about it? No doubt he was a dirty old sea dog, who thought going to sea was the ultimate pinnacle of serving in this branch of the military. It is suffice to say; he must have had his reasons. We never found out, that's for sure!

After the inspectors left, we collapsed into a heap. Our backbones felt like jelly. The DeRaps were dazed, disgruntled, disgusted and dismayed. We felt like going A.W.O.L. (Absent With Out Leave). Let's do something terrible so they will have to kick us out of the service! Let's go find that damn inspector and throw him overboard. OH, the thoughts that were flying through our heads were awful.

"Ernie," I said, "We are in deeeep dodo. That son of a gun is going for your throat, and you are going to sea, like it or not. Mark my words!"

We were two miserable, inconsolable, crushed Homo Sapiens. We spent the afternoon wallowing in our defeated feelings. Then I got madder than I have ever been. Why those stinkers; they never even made even a tiny comment about how nice and clean we had made the place look. Not so much as a smile came from any one of them. Just blank looks. What did they take us for, Robots? After we had busted our butts for weeks, making the station look like a show place. This, is the thanks we got! Thrown out to sea, damn them!

I had depleted the dictionary of foul words, as well as a few not there. It was time for a cup of boiling hot coffee, then go to the road's end to pick up Tommy at the school bus stop. We jacketed Lisa, Patti and Peter then walked them up the ramp to our car. A nice ride around the island would help. Maybe, if the wind were to blow hard enough, it would take us away from the real world and spin us into never, never land. Then I would wake up and see that the afternoon had just been a nasty dream. How I wished!

Three weeks later, Ernie received his orders. Well, I'll be damned!!! I have never seen the government work that fast before. I wondered where the dirty old inspector got his pull. Maybe he had a direct line to the Commandant in Washington.

I can't find the original orders, no doubt I threw them out, but they in effect stated Ernie was to report no later than midnight, 3 December 1962, to the Weather Cutter *Coos Bay* (WAVP - 376) at the Maine State Pier in Portland, Maine.

We had a little over two weeks to pack our goods from the light station and to get our home squared away and fixed to live in for the, very soon coming, winter months.

I will never forget the first time I entered the kitchen door of our home at Ingerson Street, after receiving Ernie's transfer orders. I met a three foot pile of sawdust sitting right in the middle of the floor. It was a good thing we were just bringing down a few things, not coming to stay.

On clear days, we were permitted to leave the station for four hours at a time. Over the past fifteen months, we tried to make our house on Vinalhaven a home, in those spare few hours. So much had to be done. I wanted a living room someday and have the children sleep upstairs. All the rooms needed painting, wallpaper or paneling. But for now we had just enough time to settle in and batten down the hatches. Ernie did get an oil furnace and a heating system installed. The rest would be forgotten, if I couldn't do it.

Doug, Barbara and their son Donnie were waiting to become the next keepers of Brown's Head L/S. On the 16th of November, we kissed Light House Service good-bye, and returned to our island home.

I forgot to mention, even though our hearts were not into gaiety, we tried to give Tommy a happy birthday party on the 11th — his eighth year. We invited several of his school friends for games, cake and ice cream.

Thanksgiving day that year was somber, I even ignored the wishbone. It was too late. After being constantly together, day and night, for the past sixteen months; how in the world could we master this separation. God only knew for how long.

At SEA — You & Me!

Ernie was, and still is, a tender hearted, ever loving husband and father. How was he going to cope being all alone, so to speak? How was I going to manage four children; one eight, another almost 5, one 2 1/2 year old and the last only 15 months old, plus taking care of the house and car, paying bills, getting groceries and on and on?

It seemed like we had just returned to the house when it was time to say so long.

Ernie drove the car to the ferry landing that dreary November 30th, 1962. When it was time for the ferry to return to the mainland, we gave each other one long hug and kiss, then he turned and ran to the boat. I almost suffocated holding back the tears. I thought, I'll be damned if I'll let him see me cry! I waved and waved until there wasn't anything to wave to. Returning to the car I flooded the seat. Any more tears and I could have rowed to the departing ferry! Not a bad idea, come to think about it.

I finally got control and said to myself, O.K. girl, this is the hand you've been dealt. Make the best of it and stop your whining. You have four healthy, beautiful children waiting. Go take care of them and hold up your end of the bargain. I drove home, ALONE!

That evening everyone was inconsolable; Tommy was sulky, Lisa, brokenhearted cried herself to sleep, Patti screamed, "I want my Daddy!" and little 15 month old Peter wobbled around the house trying to find his father. I didn't think I'd ever quiet them down.

Finally, when I was at wit's end, they slept. Now that the house was silent, it was my turn to take my frustrations out with a pillow. What a hellish night I put in. I also imagined Ernie was kicking someone's butt, about then, too. I doubted he was sleeping any better than I. No warm bod to snuggle, plus he didn't have his pillow. And I didn't imagine those shipboard bunks were very comfy. Oh shit! Why did he re-enlist?? Because we thought we would remain on LightHouse duty, stupid! How naive can one get, Polly? You gullible girl. When are you ever going to learn. The military can and does change your life overnight, without blinking an eye.

After a week or so, our lives calmed down a smidgen. I rolled out of bed at six A.M., got Tommy off to school, which was just around the corner. It was a toss up who got out of bed next, Patti, Pete or Lisa. The day began.

We heard from Ernie and our hopes soared when he said he might get home for Christmas. He also informed me that the ship sailed in January.

Later on I would write . . .

I'm the wife of a military man, making a career in the United States Coast Guard. I'm a dependent, who has to be independent. If that sounds like an odd statement, just ask any serviceman's wife, who's husband has been stationed away from home or has spent time on the high seas. I don't believe there is a more independent group to be found, than military wives!

Let me make myself clear. These past years, I wouldn't trade for all the money in the world. The experiences, good or bad, the wonderful people we've met, any inconveniences have only helped make me a better person.

Living this type of life, I've learned to stand on my own two feet, to be independent, to stand the blows and come back swinging, undaunted in the face of anything.

There were times when I did some staggering, let me tell you. I used to have horrendous bouts of bursitis, in my shoulders. That plus having to do all the work, man's and woman's, would almost floor me. Everything that went wrong would wait 'til the ship sailed, then fail. The car would not start, the furnace would breakdown, maybe we would lose our power. The kids thought this time, while father was gone, to act their worse, inside, outside or in school, or to get sick. The time I had four sick children, all at once, and ended staying up for 36 hours, was the lowest point of the month.

Planning meals, doing mounds of laundry, large rooms needed cleaning, any appointments; eye, doctor, school or otherwise, I had to take care of. Pay the bills, having not enough money to see me through to the end of the month. Keep the letters coming, blow their noses, kiss the hurts, kill those damn snakes that would come out in the spring, and slither along the foundation of the house, or worse yet, crawl near me as I hung out the clothes, and even worse to hear a neighbor scream, "Come get this snake out of my bathtub. There are no men around and, you, have to do it." "Come help me, my child is stuck in a hole and I can't get her out." Or, "Help, what do I do, domestic dogs are killing a deer out in the back field?" Another time the caller said, "What do I do, my infant is bleeding?

The Coast Guard has to take the blame, for the way I turned out. Too independent. Keeping everything on schedule. Having a spotlessly clean house AT ALL TIMES. Even years after we left the military, I was always ready for the unexpected inspection. It took the time I should have spent with my children. They were young for such a short time, I had to have a clean house and everything in its place, instead of forgetting housework and playing or reading to them. I have always felt very bad about this. But, being ready for anything was so ingrained in me, it was like what the inspectors always wrote in the logbooks, "Be safety mindful, be careful with fires." I was, and am even today, after all these years.

Postscript

Ernie endured nearly 2 years as an Engineman on the weather cutter *Coos Bay* (WAVP-376), then asked for a transfer to shore duty. He got the transfer. Not shore duty however, but another weather cutter, the *Barataria* (WAVP-381) which was docked and 'home ported' at the same Maine State Pier; Portland.

After 11 months of duty on the Barataria, he was transferred to the C. G. Base; South Portland, ME. The *Barataria* was assigned duty off the coast of Vietnam and as Ernie was the father of 4 children, he was given the option to transfer. Many other crew members of a similar circumstance, also chose not to go overseas.

Ernie worked nearly 30 months at South Portland as a "Dangerous Cargoman" inspecting crude oil tankers and harbor facilities for the "Captain-of-the-Port."

His next assignment was aboard another U.S.C.G. Cutter, the *Castle Rock* (WAVP-383) were he again worked in the engineering department as a throttleman and Engineering Watch Officer.

After years of traveling to the five North Atlantic "Weather Stations" as well as up and down the Atlantic's western shores from Iceland and Newfoundland in the north to Bermuda and further south to Cuba and Jamaica. Ernie talked about leaving the military, as if in answer, a medical problem arose deciding his dilemma for him. He was retired under a disability status. In the fall, he went to work for the State of Maine.

Ernie worked for the state 21 years. Five years as Navigational Aids Foreman, buoying Maine's larger inland lakes. Five years as the Maine Snowmobile Coordinator, coordinating the efforts of the State and Local clubs as well as developing and inspecting trails and trail signs. The previous two jobs were for the Maine Department of Conservation, Bureau of Parks and Recreation. He then worked 11 years as a State and Federal Pesticides Inspector for the Maine Pesticides Control Board (under the jurisdiction of the Maine Department of Agriculture) and the U.S. Environmental Protection Agency. He retired from state employment in July 1990.

Our family grew when Denise Diane, a tiny red head, was born on 10 September 1966 in Saco, Maine. and when Scott Fitzgerald, our surprise package was born 23 September 1970 in Portland, Maine.

Three sons and three daughters made our family complete. All six graduated from Hall Dale High School, Hallowell, Maine, where we resided 25 years.

Ernie's retirement years are busy with his being a member of the Knights of Columbus - Hallowells Council and Assembly, American Legion Post No. 6, the Spirit of America Foundation - promoting and honoring Community Volunteers, and the Local & Senior Advisory Council for Senior Spectrum - helping the aged and the infirm. He also drives his van to take seniors on day trips and outings from early spring to late fall. In his spare time he publishes a Quarterly Family NewsLetter of 30 to 50 pages which he started in July 1981. He uses his computer to type and print the newsletter, also to assemble this publication.

I spend my time making sure Ernie gets to his appointments on time, reading, and enjoying our grand children; Gabriel & Christopher DeRaps, Rebecca & Lawrence III "Buddy" Iaciofano, Megan DeRaps, Jonathan & Brandon Gilbert, Robert "Robby" Eger, III, and our last grandchild is a "surprise" brother, Samuel Ernest to Megan.

Now that you have finished reading my side of this journal, please close this book, rotate it 180 degrees and read what my husband has written as **HIS** *side of the story.*

Now that you have finished reading my side of this journal, please close this book, rotate it 180 degrees and read what my good wife has written as **HER** *side of the story.*

Sunset over Rockland, Maine with Sugar Loaf Islands off Browns Head L/S.

Browns Head at sunset showing one of two red sectors in the lantern and the lens.

The Ernest & Pauline (Fitzgerald) DeRaps family in July 1964, in front of our Vinalhaven home. Children from left to right are Patricia, Peter, Lisa, and Thomas.

The fog bell and tower at Browns Head L/S.

Sunset with lens, lantern, and top of tower at Browns Head in November 1961.

Our family was once again united at Browns Head L/S on the northwestern shore of Vinalhaven Island, the western approach to Fox Islands Thorofare.

A tranquil morning at Browns Head L/S. The lantern is only 39 feet above the water.

Sugar Loaf Islands in a light fog off Browns Head L/S.

Sunset shining up under low clouds west of Heron Neck L/S.

A "sentinel" at sunset at the Heron Neck Light Station.

The "rescue boat" was a 10-foot flatiron skiff with a 5-horsepower outboard engine.

A "golden" sunset shines on Heron Neck L/S.

Fifty foot high sea spray at Heron Neck L/S. I got wet taking this photo.

Hurricane Island and Sound from outside the lantern of Heron Neck Light Tower.

The new assignment for Ernie at Heron Neck L/S, a men only "stag" station.

Heron Neck L/S dwelling and tower.

The view of Heron Neck L/S from the ledges northeast of the station.

The motor vessel *Sunbeam* from the Maine Seacoast Missionary Society anchors off Fort Point L/S to allow its captain and crew to come ashore for a visit.

Guess who grew these great vegetables at Fort Point?

Look what Ernie built in his spare time. LETOPA, a 15-footer designed on the lines of a dory.

Morning off the Fort Point L/S, "Do Not Disturb: the calm!

Hoar-frost looking west over Penobscot Bay from Fort Point Light Tower
on an early January morning.

A late afternoon rain shower produced this beautiful rainbow over the Fort Point L/S. We didn't find any gold, but then, who needed gold when living at such a grand location?

Sunrise behind the Fort Point Fog Signal Bell Tower.

An afternoon westerly view of Fort Point Light Station including its tower and dwelling, at Cape Jellison, Stockton Springs, Maine.

The Fort Point Fog Signal Bell Tower overlooking the mouth of the Penobscot River.

Polly and Tommy looking for a ship in the fog off Fort Point.

Painting by Andrew Winter of the Monhegan Light House and Tower with the local children sledding.

Our son, Thomas, viewing the wreck of the *Cresta,* a 41-foot sailboat that grounded at Monhegan's Lobster Cove during a night-time fog. All six on board excaped the wreck safely.

A spectacular sunset, which I think looks like an eagle, over the Atlantic as seen from Monhegan Island Lighthouse.

A view of Manana Island and Monhegan Harbor from atop the Monhegan Light Tower.

One of eight "bullseyes" of the lens at Monhegan. Artist and neighbor,
Andrew Winter taking photographs inside the lantern.

Sunrise behind the Monhegan Light Tower.

Laundry day for Polly. The clothes are hung near the walkway between the tower and the dwelling.

Monhegan Island Light Tower with Pauline, Tommy, and Lisa looking out over the town.

Monhegan Island Light
Tower with the lens skirted.

Monhegan "Maine Street"
with lobster traps. The
building on the hill is the
Trefethren House, built in
the 1700s.

Monhegan Island's fresh
water supply, the light-
house is on the far hill.

USCG 40533, the 40' utility boat in Port Clyde Harbor en route to Monhegan Island.

Monhegan Island and harbor as seen from Manana Island.

The DeRaps
LightHouse Keeping
Story
in
Photographs

LightHouse Keeping

A Journal depicting our Family's life
on Three Penobscot Bay Lighthouses
and
My life at an isolated, three-man Lighthouse
South of Vinalhaven Island, Maine.

By
Ernest G. DeRaps
U. S. Coast Guard, Retired

To: Mark & Linda,
Enjoy life and your music!
Love, Uncle Ernie

Published and copyrighted by
FogHorn Publishing, Inc.
P.O. Box 68, Wells, Maine 04090
207-646-7000
www.FogHornPublishing.com

Designed by FogHorn Publishing, Inc.

Printed in the United States of America
First Printing 2006

FogHorn Publishing is a proud supporter of the lighthouse preservation efforts of the American Lighthouse Foundation

P.O. Box 889, Wells, Maine 04090
207-646-0245
www.LighthouseFoundation.org

DEDICATION

We dedicate this book to our children, their spouses, our nine grandchildren and two great grandchildren — Lily Ahna and Allythia Grace DeRaps!

FORWARD

The family of today knows a father who leaves for work in early morning and mother left to care for the toddlers. When the father's work is Light House Keeper along the Maine coast and the mother is at his side to help clean the government provided dwelling, it is a far different world. This aspect of marine history is gone. We are fortunate that Ernest and Pauline DeRaps have recorded the events of their 6 years in government owned dwellings along Penobscot Bay in Maine.

Ernest and Pauline have each provided a view of their ocean-bound day for more than a dozen years they served the United States Coast Guard and sailing craft and crews in the waters surrounding them. Although you realize the "sameness" of their day, it's too obvious how often fog, ship groundings, distress calls and delayed supply deliveries keep monotony away.

The workings of that specialized way of life is articulated with authority and humanness by Ernest. He was ever alert to the needs of others whether on sea or land. His meticulous regard for the many faceted job becomes apparent as you read his words and recognize dedication to the pathways of men and ships as well as to the honored name of the government agency he served.

The feminine/mother role is portrayed by Pauline with vibrant honesty and humor. Alone, one small son to care for as they accepted their jobs and another on the way. No close neighbors, no nearby family, no shops to visit, no daily newspaper and often the need for food supplies might be almost too much to cope with. This Irish woman had agreed to man the light house with her husband and she never turned her back on the assignment.

Any sea-loving man will relish the startling aspects of Ernest's commitment and be thankful men of his caliber have been there to oversee and protect them. Women who read Pauline's adventures in coping with unexpected Coast Guard Inspectors arrivals, weeks of fog-bound seclusion or kids out of sight behind the hill rather than over the cliff will, be impressed with her dedication and no-nonsense acceptance of a married way of life quite unlike what she expected when she and Ernie were married.

"LightHouse Keeping" and "Light HouseKeeping" is far more than a good read. The dual life of husband and wife who dedicated a dozen years of life to safeguarding sea traffic along the Maine coast reveals a unique life style. A life that modern technology now makes obsolete, but one that must be remembered. Future historians and family members will thank this delightful couple for penning their memories that will allow future generations to know the genuine determination and conviction to duty that the Light House Keeper and his family provided.

Katy

Katy Perry
Writer — Lecturer
Public Relations
9 MiddleStreet
Hallowell, Maine 04347
(207) 626-3242

— Introduction —

Would you accept the responsibilities of the very demanding job of a LightHouse Keeper?

Could you keep your sanity while living alone for weeks on an uninhabited and desolate island?

What would you do to fill in the many hours of a day, a week or a month?

These are the questions which one must face if they are to become a LightHouse Keeper at a "Stag" (men only!) station.

Another question must be faced if one is to be the Keeper at a "Family Station." Can your marriage and family survive months of isolation as well as constant togetherness?

These are some of the questions encountered by my wife, our family and me, as we maintained various Coastal Maine LightHouses during my years of Coast Guard Service.

The United States Coast Guard inducted a new recruit in October of 1955. Traveling from Belfast, Maine; after bidding good-by to his wife of four plus years and eleven month old son, the inductee was driven to the U.S. Post Office in Hallowell, Maine where he met a Recruiting Officer. From Hallowell, this recruit, and a couple others, was transported to Portland, Maine where they joined other recruits who all received a thorough physical. Those passing the physical, were individually given train tickets and orders to report to their various destinations.

Most of the inductees were sent to "Basic Training." However, one set of orders was for me and I had to report to the Coast Guard Base in Boston, Mass. Because I knew very little about the Coast Guard, I requested that I be sent to Basic Training also.

The Officer-in-Charge did not grant my request because I had been a member of the U.S. Navy in the mid-40's and went through their Basic Training Course in Bainbridge, Maryland. My stay at the C.G. Base Boston was short lived. After 3 or 4 days of testing, filling up a 'Sea Bag', etc., I was assigned my "Duty Station." Where should I travel, but back to Maine by train. My assignment sent me to the U.S. Coast Guard Base, Rockland, Maine - just a half hour drive from our home in Belfast. I did not have to report to the Base until Monday morning, so had the week end off to spend with my son, wife and her family.

My wife was very surprised to see me, as she was prepared for the worst and didn't expect to see me for some time. I didn't immediately tell her where my assigned station was to be, but told her I had been assigned to a LORAN Station in Newfoundland and would probably be there for 6 months to a year. I didn't have the heart to let her believe that for very long, but soon told her the truth. It's a wonder she didn't hit me over the head or something worse, but she was very happy to hear that I would be stationed near by.

Since my Coast Guard retirement in July of 1969, my wife Pauline and I have presented several photo slide shows depicting our Light House (L/H) days. Many of the people present at these showings have suggested that we write a book on the subject - show and tell - of those years. They also ask why we have not done so.

This manuscript is an attempt to answer the fore-going questions by word, photograph and drawing! The words are my personal impressions, except where noted or where my good wife has given of her wisdom or wit. The photographs are from our collection of personally taken colored slides and photographs. All drawings have been done by my hand!

My Side of the Story:
LightHouse Keeping
By
Ernest G. DeRaps, U.S. Coast Guard, Retired

Chapter 1 / Little Mark Island

At the Coast Guard (C.G.) Base in Rockland, Maine. I was soon taught the C.G fundamentals of watch standing. I had to learn all the essentials of keeping the LOG Book, how to stand Radio Watches, the proper procedures for standing security watches, small boat seamanship, the cleaning routines, etc. Being the oldest Seaman at the base didn't warrant any special treatment.

The Base was Headquarters for all Coast Guard operations in what was known as the "Rockland Group!" This area covered all of Penobscot Bay and the Penobscot River to the "Head of Tide" at Bangor and all offshore islands which lie south and outside of Penobscot Bay. The South-Westerly boundary was Muscongus Bay and the St. George River. The North-Easterly boundary was Deer Isle and Isle au Haut. Offshore Islands in the "Group" included all those in Penobscot Bay proper as well as the following: Matinicus Island Plantation including Matinicus Rock and its Lighthouse and to the South-West Monhegan Plantation with its Lighthouse and the sister Island of Manana with its Fog Signal Station.

Light Houses and C. G. Stations under the jurisdiction of the C.G. Rockland Group, starting at the South West boundary were as follows:
Manana Island Fog Signal Station, West of Monhegan Island
Monhegan Island Light Station (L/S), [Monhegan Plantation]
Burnt Island Life Boat Station (L.B.S.), [Georges Islands]
Marshal Point L/S, [Port Clyde]
Whitehead L/S, [Whitehead Island South of Spruce Head]
Two Bush Island L/S, [E.S.E. of Whitehead Island] Two Bush Channel
Owls Head L./S, [Owls Head - E. of Rockland Harbor]
Rockland Breakwater L/S, [South end of Rockland Harbor Breakwater]
Rockport Harbor L/S, [Privately owned]
Curtis Island L/S, [Entrance to Camden Harbor]
Grindle Point L/S, [Ferry landing at Islesboro Island]
Fort Point L/S, [Cape Jellison - Entrance to Penobscot River]
Dice Head L/S, [Privately owned at Castine]
Eagle Island L/S, [Privately owned - East-Central, Penobscot Bay]
Mark Island L/S, [Western Entrance, Deer Isle Thorofare; E. Penob. Bay]
Goose Rocks L/S, [On ledge, Eastern entrance to Fox Islands Thorofare]
Browns Head L/S, [Western entrance to Fox Islands Thorofare, Vinal-haven Island]
Heron Neck L/S, [So. East end of Green Island - So. of Vinalhaven Island]
Isle au Haut L/S, [Robinson Point; Isle au Haut - East Penobscot Bay]
Saddleback Ledge L/S, [So. entrance to Isle au Haut Bay and East Penobscot Bay]
Matinicus Rock L/S & Fog Signal/S, [Criehaven Township; Atlantic Ocean - South of Matinicus Island]

The Base was not only the Group Headquarters with a small complement of personnel and small craft (a 36 foot Motor Lifeboat, two 40 foot Utility Boats and later a 44 foot Utility/Rescue Boat), it

36 FOOT MOTOR LIFE BOAT

40 FOOT UTILITY

was also the Home Port for two larger Coast Guard vessels. The smaller of the two was the Snohomish, a sea-going Tug Boat and the larger, the Laural, a 110 foot Buoy Tender which was also used as a supply ship for the offshore island C.G. Stations, and occasionally for search and rescue.

Now on to LightHouse Keeping! I don't recall the date nor have I found records of when I was assigned the task of being a relief keeper at Little Mark Island Light/Station. I do, however, recall some of the particulars about this assignment. The Chief Warrant Officer as Commanding Officer, of the Rockland Group, one day summoned me to his office and asked if I would like to spend a few days at a Light House on Little Mark Island. He showed me its location on a chart of Penobscot Bay and told of the circumstances which prompted him to ask me to take this assignment. The assigned "Keeper" had some personal business to attend to at home, and all of the assigned Relief Keepers were on duty elsewhere. I welcomed the opportunity to spend a few days at a Light House, as I had never done so before. As a mater of fact, I do not remember ever having been inside of a light house up to that time of my life.

I gathered up a few changes of work clothes, food for a couple of days and was soon aboard a 40 foot utility boat. After the Engineman started and warmed up the two diesel engines, I helped cast off the mooring lines and the Boatswain's Mate got the vessel underway as he maneuvered away from the dock and headed out the harbor toward the Rockland Breakwater. As we rounded the Light House at the south end of the mile long breakwater, the Bo's'n set a course for Fox Island Thorofare across West Penobscot Bay. We next observed Owls Head Light Station (L/S) on our starboard side (right) and began to feel the swells and the south easterly breeze coming in from the outer bay and the Atlantic Ocean. We made good time across the bay, and were presently south of and abreast the granite day marker known as "Fiddlers Ledge."

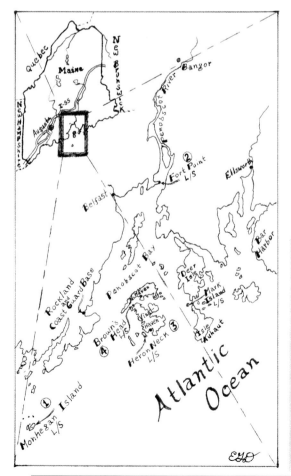

ROCKLAND BREAKWATER L/S

FIDDLER LEDGE DAYBEACON
WEST ENTRANCE
FOX ISLAND THOROFARE

We entered Fox Island Thorofare as we approached the Sugar Loaves (rock ledges) on the western side of the channel off Browns Head L/S which is located on the north west shore of Vinalhaven Island. This Thorofare is a waterway between Vinalhaven, to the south, and North Haven.

We soon passed the little town of North Haven, on our port side, and rounded Vinalhaven's Calderwood Point. As we skirted Calderwood Point, Goose Rocks L/S soon came into view. Goose Rocks was known as a "Spark Plug" light as it resembled one. It was a single steel tower with a white top and black bottom with living quarters within (men only) and it stood on a half tide ledge. Goose Rocks L/S is located at the east entrance to Fox Island Thorofare. It was here that we encountered fog. The fog didn't seem too bad at first as we could see the nearby shore. However, as we preceded east into the Eastern Bay we encountered thickening fog and the Bo's'n had to greatly reduce our speed. and resort to using dead reckoning. Visibility was at a minimum and I was asked to be the bow-watch to look for obstructions.

My first sighting was a red nun buoy off our Port bow at about 150 feet. The Bo's'n had found this aid to navigation without much difficulty. Our next course was set to bring us to Little Mark Island. My next sighting, after what seemed like a very long time, was the white of surf on a rocky shore. We carefully maneuvered north-easterly along the shore until we found the dock.

My belongings and I were off loaded and I met the waiting Light House Keeper. He escorted me to the Station and very briefly explained my duties. The fog was so thick we couldn't see the top of the tower which was attached to the dwelling. The keeper soon departed with the crew of the 40 footer and they headed back to Rockland.

I was left alone on a desolate island surrounded by a dense fog with no electricity or indoor plumbing and little to do except make routine entries in the log and care for the light and station. I found some C. G. manuals and brushed up on radio protocol and other C.G. procedures. As I recall, there was a two way, battery operated radio at the station which I had to use to call the Rockland Base at certain prescribed times. This was a safety factor, as I was the only person living on the island.

By mid-afternoon the fog lifted sufficiently for me to see some of the surrounding islands of Deer Island Thorofare. The sun was shining and being able to see a few roof-tops and a church spire off in the distance on Deer Isle in the town of Stonington lifted my spirits. I may have been alone on Little Mark Island, but people were living a short boat ride away - provided I wanted to row the boat. That evening before sunset, I went up into the light tower. I cleaned the lens and lantern windows around it then lighted the kerosene lamp which was the light source for this F. W. (Fixed White) Light. I hoped I was set for the night.

Statistics taken from the Coast Guard book "Local List of Lights and other Marine Aids" for the Atlantic Coast, Volume 1 (C.G. - 158) as released for Public Service in 1958, states the following for this L/S:

"Deer Island Thorofare Light; F. W. (Fixed White light); Resident Personnel; On west side of Mark Island, west end of thorofare at 44 degrees 08 minutes Latitude North and 68 degrees 42.2 minutes Longitude West.; Light (4th order) is 52 feet above water; the light is of 700 Candlepower and is visible for 13 miles; Light is in a White square tower attached to dwelling and was established, moved or rebuilt in 1857; BELL: group of 2 strokes every 15 seconds.

I do not recall being told about or hearing the BELL. I'm sure I have just forgotten about it in this case. However, during my short two night stay the bell was not needed once the fog lifted after my earlier arrival. I believe I returned to the Rockland Base on the third day as the keeper returned after finishing his business at home.

I must tell of a lesson I relearned while at this L/S. My first night on duty there, I lighted the kerosene lamp in the light tower after cleaning the lens and windows. An hour or so after lighting this lamp, I decided to check the tower and see if all was well. All was not well!! Evidently I had tried to get too much light out of the lamp and had turned its wick up too high. On entering the tower, I discovered a film of soot on the floor and although the lamp was still burning, it was a very dull reddish light with soot billowing up around it. Needless to say, I soon realized my mistake and corrected it by lowering the wick. I remembered my folks showing me the effects of trying to get to much light from a kerosene lamp when I was a boy on the farm - we had no electricity there. So, the next morning my first chore after breakfast and securing the light for the day, was to do a thorough clean up of the light tower and lens room. I do not recall any further significant incidents while tending Little Mark Island Light as a relief keeper. Upon my return to Coast Guard Base Rockland, I assumed my regular duties as a seaman watch-stander.

Chapter 2 / Monhegan Island L/S

My assignment to the Monhegan Island Light Station was contingent upon my wife's acceptance of this duty station, as she and our son, would be going with me. Monhegan L/S was then a "Family" Station. We had no idea what Monhegan was like as neither of us had been to the island. After questioning some of the C.G. personnel about the island and its people, checking on the duties involved as Lighthouse Keeper and doing a little historical research, we decided to accept this challenging assignment.

Upon consulting with the Commanding Officer at Group Rockland, we found that the station was reasonably equipped and we needed to take only clothing, bedding, personal effects and food to the station. Our furniture and most of our household goods had to be put into storage.

On an assigned date in August 1956, in Belfast, Maine; my wife Pauline (Polly) and I loaded our car with bag & baggage; my sea-bag, bedding, some suitcases of clothes for Pauline and our son Thomas Joseph (not quite two years old), and a few food staples. We said farewell to Pauline's family, then drove to Port Clyde (The southern terminus of State Highway #131) the embarkation point for the 10 mile voyage to Monhegan Island, its Light House and a great adventure. Read on, and join us in our experiences as LightHouse Keepers!!

At Port Clyde we transferred our baggage and food to a Coast Guard 40 foot Utility boat which would transport us to the Island. Our first born, Thomas Joseph (Named after his grandfathers, Thomas Fitzgerald and Joseph Edward DeRaps), was not the only child to journey with us to Monhegan. Pauline was expecting our second child which was due in a few months. On our arrival at the Monhegan ferry dock we discovered that we had arrived at dead low water.

It was somewhat of a test for Pauline, with her front burden, to climb up the 20 or so foot ladder to the dock. However, it was no chore for me, even with my son on my back. She made it, but in so doing, dirtied her maternity clothes with oil and scum from the ladder. I guess this incident must have endeared us to the women inhabitants who witnessed our arrival as we were accepted into the community. Island life, we were later told, can be difficult if one isn't accepted by the islanders.

Polly and Tommy were soon deposited in the Coast Guard vehicle, a four wheeled drive Dodge Power Wagon (one of the few vehicles on the island) and driven up the hill to the highest most prominent area on the island, to the Light Station (L/S).

The "Relief Keeper" who drove Polly and Tommy to the Station, soon returned and helped load our supplies into the truck. We bade so long to the 40 footer crew who headed back inshore to their Life Boat Station on Burnt Island, about four miles Sou' Sou' West of Port Clyde and Marshall Point L/S. The Relief Keeper then drove the two of us up the very steep climb to the Light Station. He stayed with us for a few days to initiate me into the routine of the station and to instruct me in the operation of the equipment.

Monhegan Island Light was a F. Fl. W., 60s (5.6s fl) or a Fixed Flashing White light - Fixed 60 seconds which was a constant light and a 5.6 second flash of white light every minute. The Light Tower stood near the center of the island at 43 degrees 45.9 minutes Latitude North and 69 degrees 19.7 minutes Longitude West and was 178 feet above water. The fixed portion of the light had 1,400 candle power and the flash (once every minute) was of 150,000 candle power which because of its height could be seen for 20 miles in clear visibility. However, it is said the light had been seen as far

away as 30 miles when there was a cloud cover to refract the light beam.

The lantern stands atop a 47 foot unpainted granite, conical tower with an attached covered way to a white dwelling. Within three miles of the island the light is obscured between west and southwest, due to the height of Monhegans' sister Island, Manana.

This L/S had a magnificent first order lens constructed of polished glass prisms set in a brass structure. It was made in France in the early 1800s. The lens was about eight feet tall and over six feet in diameter, the center portion of the lens, vertically, consisted of eight special "Bulls Eyes" which gathered the light rays and projected them in a beam of light. These bulls eyes are what made the lens appear to flash. The entire lens rotated causing the beam of light produced by each bulls eye to pass ones point of view, creating the effect of a bright 5.6 second flash of light once each minute. The lens made one complete revolution every eight minutes. The prismatic segments of the lens above and below the bulls eyes, refracted (bent) the light rays and projected them a full 360 degrees toward the horizon, creating a constant or "Fixed" light.

Prior to lighting the LIGHT each night, one half hour before sunset, there was quite a bit of preparation. Kerosene oil had to be brought from the oil / paint storage building up into the tower to the clock works / oil tank area. The oil was filtered through a chamois skin when drawn from the storage and also before being put into the small tower tank. When this tank was filled it was then closed air tight. Next to the oil tank was an air pressure tank which had to be pressurized by hand pump to force oil the six or so feet up into the lens and its Incandescent Oil Vapor (I. O. V.) burner. One had to enter the lens in order to pre-heat the vaporizer with an alcohol Bunsen torch, before lighting the mantel which was the light source. The following is why I used white cotton gloves when cleaning the lens.

The Lighthouse Keeper's Lament

O what is the bane of a lightkeeper's life
That causes him worry, struggle and strife,
That makes him use cuss words, and beat at his wife?
        It's Brasswork.

What makes him look ghastly consumptive and thin,
What robs him of health of vigor and vim,
And causes despair and drives him to sin?
        It's Brasswork.

The devil himself could never invent,
A material causing more world-wide lament,
And in Uncle Sam's service about ninety per cent,
        It's Brasswork.

The lamp in the tower, reflector and shade,
The tools and accessories pass in parade
As a matter of fact the whole outfit is made
        Of Brasswork.

The oil containers I polish until,
My poor back is broken, aching; and still
Each gallon and quart, each pint and each gill
        Is Brasswork.

I lay down to slumber all weary and sore,
I walk in my sleep, I awake with a snore
And I'm shining the knob of my bedchamber door.
        That's Brasswork.

From pillar to post, rags and polish I tote
I'm never without them, for you will please note
That even the buttons I wear on my coat
        Are Brasswork.

The machinery clockwork, and fog-signal bell
The coal hods, the dustpans, the pump in the well
Now I'll leave it to you mates, if this isn't . . . well
        Brasswork.

I dig, scrub and polish, and work with a might,
And just when I get it all shining and bright,
In comes the fog like a thief in the night:
        GOOD-BY Brasswork.

I start the next day and when noontime draws near,
A boatload of Summer visitors appear,
For no other purpose, than to smooch and besmear
        My Brasswork!!!

So it goes all the Summer, and along comes the Fall,
Comes the District machinist to overhaul
And rub dirty and greasy paws over all,
        My Brasswork.

And in the Spring, if perchance it may be,
An efficiency star is awarded to me
I open the package, and what do I SEE?
        More Brasswork.

Oh, why should the spirit of mortal be proud,
In the short span of life that he is allowed
If all the lining in every dark cloud
        Is Brasswork.

And when I have polished until I am old
And I'm taken aloft to the Heavenly fold.
Will my harp and my crown be made of pure gold?
        NO!! BRASSWORK.

By: Frederick Morong
Known by Keepers as their "Unofficial Poet Laureate."
Poem written while visiting at the Little River Light Station
Cutler, Maine

Perhaps you, our reader, have seen an Aladdin lamp with its fragile silk mantle which gives off a brilliant light when heated by a flame. The mantel used at the Monhegan L/S was about twice as large as one used in a standard household lamp. The combination of the Incandescent Oil Vaporizer and the large mantel produced 1,400 Candlepower when magnified through the fixed portion of the lens and 150,000 Candlepower when magnified through the eight bulls eyes to produce the flashing portions of the light.

One of the many questions asked about the lens, has always been, "What makes the lens rotate?" Rotation

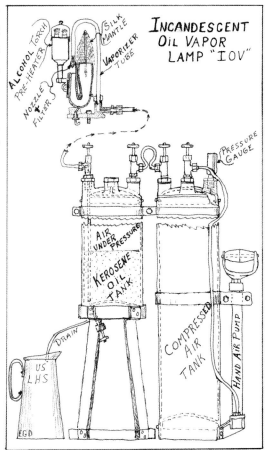

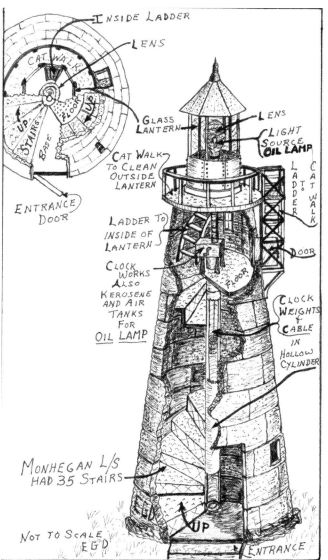

was actually provided by manpower, through the use of heavy weights and a clockworks, similar to workings of a coo-coo clock. The 35 stairs leading up to the lower level of the lens room, were placed around the inner circle of the light tower with a hollow core at the center as shown in the accompanying drawing. Within the hollow core at the tower's center were cables and weights attached to the clockworks. The gravitational downward pull of the weights made the clock work, which when operating timed the rotation of the lens. Of course someone had to overcome the gravitational pull and wind the weights up to the top of the hollow core. Guess who got that distinction? When lighted and operating, the weights had to be wound up at least every eight hours to keep the clock operating and properly rotating the lens. I used to do it about every 4 hours and let the weights drop only about half way. That meant I had to wind the ton of weights up only half way, which took about half as much time and energy. Of course I had to wind them up twice as often.

It didn't take long to meet the few business people of Monhegan. One of the first persons we met was Postmaster, Winifred (Winnie) Burton. She was the only other federal employee that I knew of, on the island. The post office also had the distinction of housing one of the three telephones on the island. Winnie's husband was one of the local fishermen during the winter lobster season and a carpenter during the summer. The majority of the men of Monhegan made their living at lobstering, but they only lobstered from January to May. Even the owners of the small local store, the two Odum brothers, lobstered during the Monhegan season. The second telephone on the island was located at their store. The third phone was at the lighthouse.

There were two inns on the island; the Island Inn, which was just up the road from the ferry dock and the Monhegan House which was located beyond the store and near the church. The church was non-denominational and pastored by Rev. Gertrude Anderson a former missionary in Burma. There was also a small sundries store which sold photographic film, post cards, souvenirs, art supplies, etc. which was located beside the post office and a small, but nice, library. The one-room school, I believe, had nine students when we arrived.

Most islanders supplemented their incomes by catering to the summer residents. Many of the homes on the island belonged to the summer residents, some of whom were artists. During the summer months the island became quite an artist colony. There were many painters but few artists. The artists we most remember were Andrew and Mary Winter, who lived just a couple houses away from the L/S. They used to play cards with us and one Christmas Andy gave us a beautiful painting of the Light House.

One day in mid January, a relief keeper came to Monhegan to take care of the station, as I had been granted leave for a short visit to the mainland. It was nearly time for the birth of a new DeRaps. Upon the arrival of the relief keeper, Polly, Tommy and I boarded the mail boat - the *Laura B* at the dock and departed, en route Belfast, Maine. We disembarked from the mail-boat at its Mainland dock in Port Clyde, got into our vehicle which had been stored in a nearby parking lot, and drove the 50 or so miles to Belfast. We were greeted by Pauline's parents Tom & Jennie Fitzgerald, where we were to spend an enjoyable but brief vacation. At least it was a vacation for me, I'm not so sure Pauline would have called it that.

On January 22nd, my 29th birthday and our 6th wedding anniversary, Polly decided in late evening that we should go to the local hospital. We arrived at the Waldo County General, shortly before midnight to find that her Dr. was not there but returning from Bangor, Maine - in a thick January fog. On his arrival, he found Polly and I sitting on a bench for two in the waiting room. He didn't take long in getting Polly into the delivery room.

At 0028 hours (28 Minutes after mid-night) on January 23, 1957 Lisa Roxane DeRaps came into the world at six lbs. three ozs. Our world has never been the same since. A week later, we were back at Monhegan L/S and into the routine of LightHouse Keeping. Of course there were a few added chores like laundering diapers and who can forget those night time feedings which never seem to come at the same hour as the time to wind up the clock weights in the tower.

Monhegan Island had a sister island known as Manana. Manana was home to a CG Fog Signal Station and its personnel, located on the west side of the island. A brown brick building housed the personnel who maintained and operated the diaphragm horn and a radio beacon. Manana Island was also home for a hermit, Ray Phillips, who lived there with his sheep and other animals; but that story comes later!

The Monhegan/Manana harbor and boat mooring area is between the two islands. Although this area was somewhat protected from the ravages of the Atlantic Ocean, it by no means was a completely safe harbor. The South Western approach to the harbor was open to the Atlantic, however, the mainland northeasterly approach was somewhat protected by a small ledge known as Smutty Nose and a little further north was Duck Island. Along the harbors edge on Manana Island was the haul-out ramp (boat slip) and boat storage shed for the Fog Signal Station's small boat. This ramp was directly across the harbor from Monhegan's only dock. Most all the islands supplies, all the vehicles and any heavy equipment were off-loaded at the Monhegan dock. It had an adjustable ramp to compensate for tide changes, but could not be lowered far enough to accommodate a landing at dead low tide. Looking from this dock, down the harbor toward the Atlantic to the southwest, one could see two small beaches. The nearest one was the swimming beach, used only by hearty souls who could brave the cold water. The second beach was known as the fish beach where the fishermen and lobstermen tended their business.

When we were stationed at the Light House, the oldest building on the Island stood on a small bluff between the two beaches. The building, known as the Trefethren's House, was built in the early 1800s and was square. It was consumed by fire after we moved from the island.

When a problem arises, who do the summer visitors seek? Usually the Light House Keeper. Located at the most prominent and visible point on the Island, made us the obvious ones to ask for help. One incident involved a young lady who, while exploring the cliffs of White Head on the northeast end of the island, fell and badly injured an ankle. Her companion didn't take to long getting to the Light House to ask for assistance. A few helping hands were forthcoming; a make-shift stretcher was put together and she was manually lugged back to the Station, where she was placed in the Station vehicle and driven to the Island Inn. The next day she was transported to the Mainland.

Another incident which we shall never forget was the loss of the sail boat *Cresta*! We housed, fed and comforted the six persons wrecked on the southwest rock ledges of Monhegan that June weekend in 1957.

A newspaper article follows:

"Six Lives, Little Else Saved in Wreck of Yawl

ROCKLAND June 30 — A yachting party of six escaped with their lives but little else early Saturday when their 41 foot yawl crashed ashore on Monhegan Island in thick weather just after dawn.

Victim of the crash was the Cresta *registered from Rye, NY., and owned by J.P. Baltzell of New York City. The yawl was under charter to a party for a cruise up the Maine coast. Loss of the*

craft was estimated at $40,000.

On board at the time of the mishap were — six people, all of New York. None of the six was injured.

Members of the party told coastguardsmen that they were trying to pick up Manana Island fog signal at the time their craft struck and had no way of knowing in the thick weather that they were near the island.

Scene of the accident was at Lobster Cove on the southwest end of Monhegan near where a tug boat crashed under similar circumstances a few years ago.

The Coast Guard icebreaker Snohomish on patrol was ordered to the scene as was the motor lifeboat from the Coast Guard's Burnt Island station but salvage efforts were unavailing because of high seas. The 64-foot harbor tug from Rockland was also dispatched to the scene of the wreck but later ordered back when it became apparent that the yawl could not be saved.

Salvage crews from Boothbay Harbor today recovered the yawl's engine, generator and some navigational gear."

The foregoing incident is just another saga in the life of a LightHouse Keeper! I might add, this one had a happy ending!!

The following letter written by me to the Maine Coast Fisherman, dated 7 September 1957 tells about happenings up until that time.

Mr. Owen Smith
Maine Coast Fisherman
Camden, Maine

Your card, addressed to this station and to Henley Day (the former Keeper), has prompted this letter. We've been intending to write you for some time. My secretary, the Mrs., generally takes care of unofficial correspondence but guess it's up to me this time.

First of all, Henley is now a happy civilian, or seemingly so. He has a home here at Monhegan and lobsters with the rest of the men during the open season. This summer he has been the assistant road commissioner and perpetually busy doing repairs on the homes of summer residents. Just this morning I saw him bringing his boat back to its winter mooring, from repairs and an overhaul inshore.

We were assigned this station last August, and in this short year we have had our share of excitement. We had been here less than a month when word was received that a young lady had been hurt on the back side of the island. First aid was rendered and a stretcher improvised for the one-half mile carry to the nearest semblance of a road, where the Coast Guard truck was used to drive her to the Inn. A visiting doctor found broken bones in her foot as well as a badly sprained ankle. She was taken inshore next morning via an airplane with floats.

Upon my request, the Group Commander of Rockland sent us a stretcher shortly after this incident and fortunately it has sat in storage since.

We then settled into a routine and readied the station for winter. The usual chore of putting up storm windows and storing screens, filling the coal bin and finding drafty doors, windows, etc., to which was applied weather stripping. Guess we got things pretty well buttoned up as we were very comfortable through all the weather the old Atlantic threw at us.

Came Christmas, and we were off to Belfast. We stayed with the wife's folks and they were very pleased to have their only grandson home for the holiday. The morning after Christmas I had to return to Monhegan, so I bid good-bye to the Mrs. and Tommy Joe, my son, who stayed for a little longer visit.

January came, and once again Monhegan Lobstermen took to their boats. The Monhegan lobster

season had begun. But, more important we had a beautiful daughter born January 23rd in Belfast. In early February we were all together again, at home on Monhegan.

We had a good spring, seemed good to get out of doors and clean up for summer. Now it's almost gone. Where, oh where, did the time go? With the many visitors to see the light, plus our having the best view of town from our front yard and the usual cleaning and painting of the station, we had a very enjoyably busy summer.

Of course we won't forget our most exciting day of all, June 29th, when the Cresta, *a 41 foot yacht, came aground at Lobster Cove. All six persons aboard were saved, but the vessel was a total loss.*

The cycle has run its course, and now it's back to the storm windows, coal bin and weather stripping. Wonder what's in store for the coming year? Well, the big talk concerning Monhegan Island L/S, is electrification and automation. An added responsibility for the men at Manana Fog Signal/Radio Beacon Station. They will probably have the generators and switches over there. Of course there will be a small standby generator here in the tower in case the cable from Manana gets broken or out of order. All of this will mean good-bye to Monhegan for us, so we hope they take their time.

We shall miss Monhegan, and our many wonderful friends on the island. The folks here are very nice and have been kind to us. They help us whenever they can and have made us feel as though we have always belonged here.

In closing, I would like to ask any of the many keepers to drop us a note: especially the four or five keepers in New England who are still operating I. O. V. (Incandescent Oil Vapor) lights. Any operating tricks that may help me keep this old timer lighted and operating well, will be appreciated.

The DeRAPS of Monhegan Light
Ernie, Polly, Tommy Joe & Lisa Roxane

We occasionally had off-island visitors. Family members who came to see us for short visits were: Polly's Dad and Mom, Tom and Jennie Fitzgerald of Belfast, Maine.; my Dad, Joseph Edward DeRaps of Winslow, Maine.; my oldest sister Bernadette Muzeroll and her son Peter of Waterville, Maine.; and two of Pauline's cousins Alice Sanborn & Estelle Baird, both from Lewiston, Maine.

On several occasions we were visited by members of the Maine Seacoast Missionary Society who travel the coast in "God's Tugboat," the M/V *Sunbeam*. It was always a pleasure to greet these folks who did so much good along the coast serving isolated island communities. Their services were many. Sick islanders were many times ferried to the mainland and a hospital when most small fishing craft were unable to negotiate heavy weather and high seas. These folks were often the only religious affiliation that many islanders had.

This society has been an important part of the history of the Maine island communities for nearly 90 years. Its present vessel, *Sunbeam IV* now carries ministers to the islands and the society's many craft through the years have served as seagoing ambulances, clinic, library, school and even Santa Claus.

This Mission Society was founded in1905 by two brothers, Alexander and Angus MacDonald of Bar Harbor, Maine. The first ship was a 26 foot Friendship sloop named *Hope*, and the Rev. Henry White was the first minister. He later became pastor at a church in Owls Head near Rockland.

In 1906, a 38 foot yacht was given to the Society by an Episcopal Bishop who was a summer res-

ident of Seal Harbor, the Right Reverend Alexander Mackey-Smith. This vessel was named the *Morning Star* and used until 1912 when she was replaced by the first *Sunbeam*. The first *Sunbeam* was a gift from Mrs. John S. Kennedy, a summer visitor to Bar Harbor. Now *Sunbeam IV* is serving the coastal islands. She was built in 1964 and is an all-steel 65 foot vessel. To many vacationing on Maine waters, this is just one more craft, but to the islanders of Maine her appearance is a welcome sight.

One day just prior to Christmas we heard an airplane flying low over the light house, buzzing us. It took us a few minutes to realize what was happening. We were being visited by Edward Rowe Snow, the "Flying Santa" of Massachusetts. Mr. Snow made it a practice to deliver Christmas gifts to isolated Lighthouse personnel each year. In order to make it more personal and much less time consuming, he used to fly his gifts to each Light House.

E. R. Snow story:

Before leaving this chapter on Monhegan I'll comment about Manana Island's Hermit. I met him only once, but saw him many times during our tour of duty at Monhegan L/S. We saw him from "afar," the Light House, through binoculars. No, we weren't spying on him. We had to occasionally check the vicinity for overdue vessels, etc, and we had to check beyond Manana. We could see his insubstantial residence which he shared with a few sheep and other animals. If my memory serves me, he had stated that it takes about 3 years to gather enough driftwood to add a new room to his structure. The sheep were his major but meager means of finance. A former Chemical Engineer from New York City, he retreated to the solitude of Manana Island during the great depression of the 1930s.

The Manana Island Fog Signal Station.

Chapter 3 / Fort Point L/S

One bright, sunny day while on leave from our duties at Monhegan Island L/S, in the summer of 1957, Polly and I decided to visit a place she had never been. We were visiting her folks in Belfast and thought a picnic would be nice. But where should we venture? I remembered that as a young-ster, my folks used to drive down from our little farm in Palmyra, Maine, to the then falling down ruins of some docks and a railhead on Cape Jellison on the eastern shore of Stockton Harbor. It seemed like a nice spot to have a picnic with the children, and was not too far to travel.

When my folks journeyed there in the late 1930s, we used to make it an overnight camping stay, usually on a holiday weekend. It was quite a trip in those days, but usually well enjoyed. My dad espe-cially enjoyed it, because he missed his childhood years when he lived in the maritime provinces of Labrador along the Gulf of St. Lawrence. He liked to dig clams and catch salt water fish. These once or twice a year trips were a welcome treat after working long hours in the dye house of a Pittsfield woolen mill to support his large family of 14 children. The trip to the shore took several hours in those days, especially if we had one or two flat tires along the way - tires and tubes during the depression years were not only expensive but hard to find. A flat tire required patching and many strokes of a tire pump to inflate it again. Because of the stress of the trip, once we got there we did not explore beyond a walking distance and did not use the car until it was time to return home. Consequently, we never discovered a beautiful location known as Fort Point only a few miles further east on the Cape, nor did we discover the Light House there.

Polly and I decided that Cape Jellison would be the destination for our picnic. We had a great time, once I found the new road leading to the old docks and the railhead. We spent the good part of the day exploring the remains of the docks with the children. As we were packing up our picnic remains, I suggested we explore the Cape by car, something I had never done before. Somehow, I recalled seeing nautical charts that showed a Light House out on the tip of Fort Point, so we decided to try to find it. What a delightful spot we found, the Light House on the edge of a rather high cliff, overlooking the north-eastern por-tion of Penobscot Bay and the mouth of the Penobscot River. The views made our day, but the tired children told us we had to find them a bed. We returned to Belfast and at the end of my leave returned to our duties at Monhegan Island L/S.

WINTER AT FORT POINT
LOW TIDE-UPPER PENOBSCOT BAY

FOG-BELL FORT POINT L/S

In early December, we received word that the Keeper of Fort Point L/S, Mr. Ernest Mathie had suddenly passed away. Much to our surprise, Pauline and I were asked if we would take over the duties there. We were delighted. As much as we had enjoyed life at Monhegan and the people there, it would be nice to be on the mainland once again, and only about 15 miles to Polly's folks

home in Belfast.

I received orders dated 5 December 1957 from "COMMANDER Coast Guard Group Rockland, Maine" which read: "1. Having been assigned by proper authority to duty at FORT POINT LIGHT STATION. You are hereby assigned one set of Government quarters at subject station for the occupancy of yourself and dependents, effective 5 December 1957." Signed by H. N. Litchfield; Commander - Rockland Group.

This would be our second move while on Coast Guard Duty and now we had two children. Prior to these moves, Pauline and I had lived in several places, most of them in Maine. After our marriage in Belfast, we lived for a short while in Fairfield. Our second residence was a two room apartment in Waterville. We moved to the third floor apartment at her folks home in Belfast. I obtained a job with the U.S. Internal Revenue Service in Washington, DC. as the National IRS Headquarters Photographer. We had moved three times During our 28 months stay in D.C., when I received a "Reduction in Force" (R.I.F.) notice. No longer employed, we returned to Maine living first in Veazie, then moving to Old Town and back to Belfast. Thomas Joseph, our first born, was delivered at the Eastern Maine General Hospital in Bangor while we were living in Veazie. We were living in Belfast when I enlisted in the Coast Guard in 1955.

We had packing and moving down to a science, however there were a few hitches. This would be only our second move over the ocean. Boxes had to be more sturdy than usual and packing had to possibly withstand more tossing about. The ocean is very fickle and at times gets very rough, giving no quarter.

We were relieved of our duties at Monhegan and traveled directly to our new duty station at Fort Point L/S. We had to get our household furniture out of storage for use, until such time as the C.G. sent us new furnishings. We arrived at the Light House just one week before Christmas. On Christmas Day we were reasonably settled, had a tree up and decorated, also gifts were already wrapped and we served Christmas dinner with all the fixings to Polly's Mom and Dad.

Checking through records, newspaper clippings and other sources, I have found the following information about Fort Point L/S:

Light list #135 indicates Fort Point Light was a F. W. (Fixed White) light with resident personnel which stands on the west side of the mouth of the Penobscot River at 44 degrees 28 minutes north latitude and 68 degrees 48.7 minutes west longitude. The light stands 88 feet above water producing 4,500 candlepower which is visible for 15 miles in clear weather. In 1935 the old oil lamp was discontinued and a new I.O.V. light source installed. The Light was electrified in June 1950 and automated in late September, 1988. The fourth order lens (made in Paris, France) was atop a white square tower connected to a dwelling built in 1836 and reconstructed in 1857. A short distance north east of these structures is a bell tower constructed in 1891. This tower contained a brass and steel clockworks mechanism activated by a slowly falling 2000 pound weight. The weight had to be manually raised to the height of the tower through the use of pulleys (giving a mechanical advantage) and a winding device. The clock-works were designed to strike a 1,200 pound liberty bell which during poor visibility was struck once every 20 seconds. The bell has since been replaced by an electrically-operated horn placed on the lens tower. This Light House was first constructed during the Presidency of Andrew Jackson and originally had only 3,000 candlepower.

The first Keeper assigned was William Clewley, on Sept. 8, 1836, others who followed were: John Odom (became Keeper in1853), Henry Stowell, Hiram Grant (became Keeper in 1882), Adelbert Webster, Captain John Thurston, E. S. Ferren, Captain Arthur Mitchell and Ernest Mathie. All of

these men were members of the United States Light House Service. In 1939, the Coast Guard took over this Service.

Light House Service men, were allowed by the Coast Guard, to continue their duties until such time as they retired. Captain Arthur Mitchell was assigned Keeper of Fort Point L/S, in 1929, shortly after his marriage, and stayed as keeper of this L/S for 21 years. He retired in 1950 at age 70. Mr. Mathie relieved Captain Mitchell and was Keeper here until he passed away in 1957.

I was the first Coast Guardsman to take over this station as Officer in Charge. My replacement was Robert Kenney, next came Wayne McGraw. They were followed by several others. To my knowledge, the final Keeper and Officer-in-Charge of Fort Point L/S for years prior to its being automated, was Larry Baum.

There is one odd fact about the light tower. Although the tower is surfaced with brick and SQUARE on the outside, it is ROUND on the inside. It has circular steel stairs leading up to the lens level. This upper area is known as the lantern, as it is surrounded by glass panels.

When my family and I moved to Fort Point, we weren't aware of the history surrounding us, but Pauline soon uncovered much of it. In 1626 the English set up a trading post at the mouth of the Penobscot River near here. The French and Indians attacked it often with great ferocity. After only ten years the post was abandoned. In 1640 a crude fortification was built and was more successful. By 1740 there were hundreds of people living in the area. In 1755 Indian attacks were at their peak and war was declared. The next notable event in the history of this region was the construction of a small fortification started by Governor Thomas Pownal of Massachusetts in 1759, called Fort Pownal. The foundation is just north of the present Light House.

During our tenure at Fort Point L/S, we received notice that the U.S. Government was interested in disposing of some of its vast land holdings. We contacted what was then the "Maine State Park Commission," directed by Lawrence Stuart, in Augusta. Although purchase funds were very limited and State budgets tight, eventually, part of the land adjacent to the Light Station was purchased by the State. The land which was purchased contained the area where about 200 years previously, Fort Pownal was constructed. This area is presently a rather unique Memorial. More land was later purchased and is now a very nice State Park with a 200-foot fishing pier with a floating dock and a picnic area with tables and benches. One can readily explore the ruins, moats and breastworks of old Fort Pownal at Maine's Fort Point State Park.

Also during our stay at Fort Point L/S, I was allowed sufficient time off from my duties to become Scoutmaster of a nearby Boy Scout Troop which was sponsored by the local American Legion Post. This, in a small way, allowed me to repay my debt to the Boy Scout movement which helped me as a boy become a responsible adult. When I was assigned to my next duty station, Heron Neck L/S, the Scouts and their parents gave my family a going away party and presented me with a sizable "Money Tree." The money came in very handy and helped pay the expenses of moving my family, and getting settled in a house we rented in Stockton Springs. The local people called the place, "Shadow Lane" as the drive was quite long and lined with many large maple trees. We called it, "The Captain's House."

Letterhead of "Maine Coast Fisherman"
Spring 1958
Hello Readers of MCF:

Will take a few minutes off from my book work and routine duties, to wish all readers a happy and prosperous New Year. Sorry we're late with the wishes; but, does anyone have an automatic, push button device for quick, easy and efficient transfer of a family of four from Monhegan Island to Fort Point L/S in Stockton Springs, Maine? The distance isn't so great, but have you tried packing lately? How does one small family accumulate so much in a year or two?

My wife and I, along with many others, were very sorry to hear of the death of Mr. Ernest Mathie, keeper at Fort Point L/S. Mr. Mathie passed away December 3 after a very short illness. I'm sure we will all miss reading the frequent letters sent in by him. Mrs. Mathie is spending the winter with her daughter in Wisconsin.

Having been assigned this station, we're happy to be on the mainland, especially for the winter, but shall miss Monhegan and all our friends. The bustle of the little Plantation with the fellows out lobstering, the gatherings at the dock at mail-boat time and friends at the Lighthouse for an evening of cribbage or canasta, is certainly in contrast to our just seeing the mailman once a day and an occasional ship going by. We did however, have a guest last week, Mr. Norman Woodard a 'Sea and Shore Warden' was corralled and invited in for coffee.

We're getting settled gradually, but every day something new seems to show up. I'll start doing some job and barely get to work when my wife finds more for me to do. Pictures to be hung, this or that done. Everything is in good shape here at the station; but like all women, my wife sees changes to be made and painting to be done.

Want to thank the MCF (Maine Coast Fisherman) staff for the fine articles on boat building. I got so interested in them while on Monhegan that I decided to design and build my own. She is a modified dory design, with a deeper bow and V bottom. She is constructed of 3/8" marine plywood over 1 inch spruce and oak frames jkkk khkhk 12p Excuse the last phrase; Tommy, my 3 year old son noticed this letter in the typewriter while I was reading the day's mail! Says he wants to learn to type! Back to my boat again; she has an oak keel, oak stringers and is about 15 1/2 feet in length. I plan to use a 10 HP outboard on her in a built-in well. This is my first attempt at boat building, so I'm anxious to get her finished and into the water so I can see how she handles. Another reason for my anxiety is the fact that I designed her myself. At the present, she's in my old work shop on Monhegan, didn't have room to bring her in when we came.

The Mrs. and I want to extend an invitation to all readers to drop in and see us. It only takes a couple of minutes to heat water, and we have a good supply of coffee on hand.

"Ernie" DeRaps and Family

Chapter 4 / Heron Neck L/S

I remember my first view of Heron Neck L/S, from a Coast Guard 40 foot utility boat. I was being transported there to my new assignment. We had embarked at the C.G. Base in Rockland on a bright, sunny day. Traveling southeasterly across Penobscot Bay and the Atlantic Ocean, south of Vinalhaven Island and the Hurricane Islands we approached Green Island and the Light House from the south west, but to the east of Duck Ledges. The Bo's'n steered us around the eastern head of Heron Neck and into Deep Cove on the southeast side of Green Island.

Upon arrival at the boat slip in Deep Cove, we were met by Kermit Scarborough, Bo's'ns Mate First Class, the Officer-in-Charge, who had come to greet us and welcome me aboard my new duty station. This station was a STAG (men only) station, with three of us assigned. I was in charge of Engineering as I held the rank of Engineman 2nd Class. The third member of our crew was James Wood a Fireman, striking for Engineman. We were a fair representation of the Atlantic coast as Kermit hailed from Norfalk, VA. and originally from Cape Hatteras, NC.; Jim was from Miami, FL. and I am from Central Maine (a Maine-iac), born in Palmyra and schooled in Pittsfield. You see there was represented; a Reb., one person from the Mason-Dixon and a Damned Yankee. No revolution though, we were United States Coast Guardsmen!

The hardest part of this new assignment was leaving my family, Pauline my wife and our two children. However, when in the service, one does as he or she is ordered to do.

Statistics for Heron Neck L/S were as follows: The light was a "F.R., W. sector (Fixed RED, with a WHITE sector) was number 137 on the "Local List of Lights" and used an electric bulb for the light source. The Station had Resident Personnel and was located on the East side of the entrance to Hurricane Sound at 44 degrees 01.5 minutes Latitude North and 68 degrees 51.7 minutes Longitude West. The "Light" stood 92 feet above water in its cylindrical white tower which was connected to the dwelling.. The lens's red sector was of 1,000 candle power visible in fair weather for 14 miles and the white sector of the light was of 4,500 candle power and could be seen for 15 miles.

HERON NECK L/S
- GREEN ISLAND

The white sector was from 030 degrees to 063 degrees. The light was obscured, close-to, between 312 degrees and 318 degrees. A fog signal SIREN outside the lantern on the light tower produced 1 blast of 3 seconds duration every 30 seconds, when turned on in foul weather. The light tower and siren were just a short distance outside my bedroom, consequently when the siren was operating, due to foggy weather, I didn't get much sleep with its vibration and loud wailing sound. The dwelling and tower were constructed in 1854 on the edge of a headland 30 to 40 feet above the bay's high water line. Many a southeast storm deposited tons of salt spray and occasionally green water on the tower and dwelling which required frequent painting. In good weather, however, the views were wonderful and we often witnessed spectacular sunrises and sunsets. I have captured a few photos which illustrate the views. My very first oil painting, which I started during a hospital stay at Staten Island NY., and eventually completed, was a view of Heron Neck L/S sitting on its high bluff with ominous storm clouds brewing in the background.

There was no potable water source at the station, no wells. The only source of fresh water was the station's water cisterns which were located in the basement of the dwelling. Water was collected from the dwelling roof and directed into the cisterns. Therefore, we had to keep a close eye on our use of water and it had to be tested for purity each month. When the bacteria count began to get too high, we were directed to put a small amount of Clorox bleach into the water. That doesn't sound very appetizing, but when boiled and in a pot of tea or cup of coffee, we managed to survive. Our only electricity at the station, was produced by two generators. One at a time, run as needed, with the second on stand-by.

Part of our duty, as with all Coast Guard Stations, was our constant watch for vessels in distress or need of help. When the Station was sufficiently manned, we stood assigned watches around the clock and had duty lists to keep ourselves busy. The daily routines still come to mind after nearly 35 years away from that Station. The midnight to 8 A.M. watch made routine rounds of buildings and had to record weather, etc. in the log each hour. He usually cooked breakfast for all on board prior to the raising of the colors (Old Glory) at 8 A.M. After breakfast and cleaning the dishes, the mid-

watch was allowed 4 hours of rest. The 8 A.M. to 4 P.M. watch was responsible for all recordings in the log book during his watch, cleaning of the communal portion of the dwelling, phoning reports to C.G. Base Rockland and any other jobs assigned by the Officer-in-Charge.

Most noon meals were catch as you can, do for yourself and be sure to clean up any mess you might make. Most evening meals were communal and they liked my cooking, when I cooked I knew what was in the pot! My Boy Scout training was a great help at meal times. The 4 P.M. to Midnight watch was responsible for lowering old glory 1/2 hour before sunset, turning the light on in the tower, making the 8 P.M. report to Group Rockland and was keeper of the log books 'til relieved at midnight.

BROWNS HEAD L/S
VINALHAVEN ISLAND

Of course we all had work to accomplish on our watches during most daylight hours. It seemed something always had to be scraped and painted (I guess it's an old Navy/Coast Guard saying; "If it don't move - PAINT IT!") The buildings had to be maintained, the furnace had to be fueled and coal brought up over the hill from the boat landing, the generators were my responsibility as was the boat winch down at the boat house, all needed routine maintenance, water depths in the cisterns had to be taken and recorded weekly if not more often, the telephone lines had to be checked frequently due to the strong winds which often blew. I spent much of my off-duty time writing letters and studying C.G. Correspondence courses, about the only way to earn a rate in the C.G. I also spent some time making model boats and replicas of some C.G. small-craft and did a little sketching. When things got too close or demanding, I could take solitary nature walks in the nearby woods or find work to do in solitude. (Even to this day, I find solace and solitude in nature and a healing comfort in God.)

We were more fortunate than some island stations, as we had a telephone and could communicate with Rockland C.G. Base and others as needed. An above ground telephone line came to the station from the north end of Green Island after crossing "The Reach" via underwater cable from Vinalhaven Island. The Vinalhaven Island telephone connected to an underwater cable from North Haven across the "Fox Island Thorofare" and a very much longer underwater cable (about 5.5 nautical miles) from North Haven to Owls Head on the Mainland, near Rockland.

There were times when only one of us was at the station. With one person on leave or off-duty status, that left only two people to man the station, to carry out watches and routine duties. At times we needed groceries, mail, etc., so one person had to leave the station to get them. Our usual means of obtaining mail and groceries, was to boat into the town of Vinalhaven. The station was assigned a 16 foot open small-boat and a 10 H.P. outboard motor, to be used for these errands and other chores around the station. Our trips to Vinalhaven were not too frequent, especially during the winter months. The reason being, that we had to travel around Green Island's easterly point of land north of Deep Cove, known as "Boiler Point"! Our fiberglass craft was quite seaworthy and could stay afloat in some pretty heavy weather. However, we were ordered not to take unnecessary risks and to keep a sharp eye on both the weather and the sea when using this boat.

Occasionally, supplies were needed when we couldn't use our small boat due to extended bad weather and angry seas. We did have an alternate way to get food supplies; a walk across Green Island, a mile or so to a lobster pound where we borrowed a small row boat to cross a water channel to Vinalhaven Island.

One such foul weather day when walking across Green Island to row to Vinalhaven for food supplies, I came across a very small grave site. It was evidently the burial site of the island settlers for whom the island was named, Mr. and Mrs. Green. I remember there were separate stones for both the Mr. and the Mrs. I believe there was another stone but don't remember much about it. What I have never forgotten, is the epitaph on Mr. Green's grave stone which read:

Stop my friend, as you pass by,
          as you are now, so once was I.

As I am now, so you must be,
          prepare for death, then follow me.

Chapter 5 / Browns Head L/S

On 8 July, 1961, Pauline and I, our children; Thomas, Lisa, and Patricia reported for duty at Brown's Head Light Station. This was a "family" LightHouse, a chance for us to be a FAMILY once again as I was designated the Officer-in-Charge. Our move also allowed us as a family, to attend church services more frequently. There was a missionary Catholic Church at North Haven which was a short drive and a shorter ferry ride away. We could drive to the roads end, park the vehicle, board a small scow-ferry to cross Fox Island Thorofare to the town of North Haven and walk a short distance to the church. A priest came by boat from Stonington, Maine to officiate at the Holy Mass.

We were not exactly unfamiliar with Brown's Head Light Station, as we had visited several times to see the former keeper and his family. This was the second time we happened to be assigned a station we had previously visited, quite unlike our assignment to Monhegan Island L/S and my appointment to Heron Neck L/S. It's rather nice to know where your going and what to expect in the way of living accommodations. We felt sure we were going to like living at our newly assigned station, even if it was very, very close to the bay waters.

This is probably a good time to state that, of the three stations at which our family lived, this one was the closest to the water's edge. So close in fact that many a storm sent spray flying up to the second story windows of the dwelling. The building and its foundation were actually bolted to the stone cliffs edge. The uphill portion of the basement was merely a crawl space where the stone rose nearly to the floor above.

What were the Light List statistics for Brown's Head L/S? According to my "1958" copy of the LIGHT LIST, they were as follows:

Browns Head Light — F. W., 2 R. sectors (Fixed White, 2 Red sectors)   Resident Personnel — On northwest point of Vinalhaven Island, west entrance to Fox Islands Thorofare — 44 deg. 06.7 minutes. North and 68 deg. 54.6 minutes West —The light is 39 feet above mean high water, the white sector has 3,000 candlepower and the red has 600 candlepower and can be seen 11 miles. The light is atop a white cylindrical tower connected to a dwelling, first built in 1832, reconstructed in 1857. The light shows two red sectors from 001 deg's to 050 deg's and from 061 deg's to 091 deg's with fairway between. There is also a bell which delivers 1 stroke, 20 seconds silence; group of 2 strokes, 20 seconds silence.

One could get to the station either by water, air or land. Arriving by boat, there was no dock or wharf to deposit supplies or personnel on. Someone from the station had to launch a small rowboat (double-ended peapod) from the boathouse and transfer personnel and or supplies on the water. There was a rather steep ramp (boat-slip) from the boathouse down into the water and a gasoline engine driven winch, to haul the peapod back up the boat slip and into the boathouse.

Arrival and departure by air was either by helicopter, which could land up on the hill behind the station, by seaplane or by light plane which could land at a small airfield southwest of Seal Bay.

One could also arrive by land vehicle over rough, twisting roads from the town of Vinalhaven which is 7 or 8 miles away at the south east end of the island. This of course would be after a 1 and 1/2 hour ferry trip from the mainland, departing from Rockland. Another route utilized to arrive by land vehicle, via a ferry ride from Rockland to North Haven and another ferry, an un-motorized scow maneuvered by a small lobster type boat, from North Haven across the Fox Islands Thorofare to the northern terminus of the Vinalhaven road system.

You could not drive directly to the dwelling. Only to the station garage which was nearly atop the hill overlooking the light and bell towers, the dwelling and West Penobscot Bay. Across the bay were the communities of Rockland, Rockport and Camden, as well as the Camden Hills and the State Park.

Descending to the station and dwelling, one had to walk 150 or so feet down a rather steep board-cleated ramp with an attached railing to get to a small deck area next to the dwelling with its attached light tower and the detached bell tower.

The dwelling's kitchen entrance was to the left, the bell tower was to the right and the roof of the boathouse was just below. A second ramp of heavy planking went about 25 feet to the boat house and extended into the bay. The lower portion paralleled dual, well greased, skid timbers from the boathouse down into the water. This 'boat-slip' was used to slide the station row boat in and out of the water. The ramp below the boathouse, was at times nearly covered by a high tide, but had probably 30 feet exposed at low water. It is somewhat hard to remember all the details of these stations after 30 plus years. Some details are more vivid than others.

One vivid memory is, my assisting 6-year-old Thomas, up the ramp to the station truck on a snowy, blowy, westerly-wind morning in two feet of snow so we could drive the mile to our road-head to meet his school bus at the main road. I was afraid Tommy might get blown away going up that hill, so tied a hemp line around our waists. Tommy thought it great fun and said he would certainly have something to tell his teacher and classmates, this snowy day. I guess Pauline liked the idea, as she congratulated me upon my return.

Another memory, is of the great seafood feasts we had while stationed here. There was a rather long, sheltered cove over the hill and east of the station. At low tide the mud flats would yield a sizable hod full of steamer clams if one worked hard enough. The cove gave up a few flounder from time to time, as time and work schedules permitted. I also fished 4 or 5 lobster traps within this sheltered cove. You couldn't buy these delicious eatables any fresher. This cove is also where I moored my personal, home built, outboard driven, modified dory and beached my 8 foot (home built) punt. My "dory" we had named *Litopa*, in honor of our children - Lisa, Tommy and my better-half, Pauline. After completing my punt, we had added two more youngsters to the family, so I named the punt PePa, in honor of our daughter Patricia and a new son Peter.

While stationed here, I was instructed to clear an area atop the hill so that helicopters could land; a heliport! As I recall, the first time a helicopter landed, it brought a U.S. Public Health doctor., to give Pauline, the children and me, influenza shots. I believe the second landing, brought three inspectors from the First Coast Guard District of Boston, MA. The ones who decided I needed to get some sea duty as I had been too long on lighthouses and shore duty.

Chapter 6 / Off to SEA

Having been stationed at Browns Head L/S for 16 months and enjoying FAMILY life, it was quite a shock when the Eastern Inspection team told me I had to go to sea. I knew a Coast Guardsman had to have a period of "Sea Duty" before attaining the higher Petty Officer rates. However, Pauline and I were quite content with my Second Class Petty Officer rating and pay status, especially when we were able to live as a family.

I knew many Guardsmen who served their "Sea Duty" time, on small vessels such as the buoy tenders, etc., vessels that were based at shore facilities. Personnel on these vessels were able to see their families quite frequently and usually were never away from port more than a few days at a time. An assignment to one of these vessels would have suited me fine., however, this was not to be. The Rockland Group Commander told me that I would be relieved of duty at Browns Head L/S on 16 November, 1962 and I was granted annual leave (time off) to help my family get settled in our Vinalhaven home, starting the next day.

My orders of transfer stated that I must report on board the U.S. Coast Guard Cutter *Coos Bay* (WAVP 376) at Maine State Pier, Portland, Maine; no later than midnight 3 December 1962.

I was to serve on board a Weather Cutter whose home port was at the Maine State Pier in Portland, Maine. These vessels were alternately sent into the North Atlantic Ocean assigned to 21 days on a weather station (several plotted 10 square mile areas) to gather weather information and act as beacons for transatlantic aircraft and shipping. Their usual routine was a month at dock in port, then a month at sea. Occasionally one was sent to an in-port other than its home-port, consequently, the ship was away from its home port for three months.

Life aboard a U.S.C.G. Weather Cutter is another story and may be another book!

Correspondence:

Having been a Lighthouse keeper in the past and still very much interested in lighthouses and their demise, my wife and I subscribe to a small publication known as the *Lighthouse Digest*. We received our first copy in May 1992 (a complimentary issue) and subsequently subscribed to it. That very first issue had an aerial photograph of Heron Neck Light Station on its cover and a story about the U. S. Coast Guard finding a lessee to restore the fire damaged structure. The Coast Guard had considered the possible demolition of the station which was on the National List of Historic Places. This story certainly interested me as I had tended that light as a keeper and Engineering Officer.

The *Lighthouse Digest* helps keep Pauline and me informed of lighthouse happenings throughout the United States and now as the "International Lighthouse Magazine," it covers the world lighthouse news. We both have strong feelings about the demise of the nation's long serving lighthouses, their automation and the loss of personnel to man and maintain these stations. Human senses can not be replaced by automated machinery or electronic gadgetry. The personal judgment of a lighthouse keeper (a person) can not be equaled or duplicated by machinery or electronics.

The February 1994 Issue of the *Lighthouse Digest* had a winning photograph of Monhegan Island Light Tower and this prompted me to initiate the following correspondence:

Lighthouse Digest
P.O. Box 68
Wells, Maine 04090

26 February, 1994

Lighthouse Digest Readers:

As a retired Coast Guardsman, Officer-in-Charge and Keeper of three Maine Light House Stations and Engineman in Charge of another, I would like to say hello to all readers of your informative digest. I am presently working on a book about my past Light House duties and would appreciate hearing from any other present or former Light House Keepers.

My wife and I were very pleased to see in the Lighthouse Digest *February 1994 Issue, that a photo of Monhegan Island Light House was awarded First Place. The photo brings back many fond memories of our 16 month tour of duty there. If memory serves me, we were the last 'full-time' Family keepers stationed there. Our second child was born during our tenure at Monhegan. As a matter of fact, three of our six children were born while we served as Light House Keepers.*

I have included a Resume of Service with this brief letter and a poem which I believe sums up well, a big part of a Light House Keepers' duties.

My wife Pauline and I look forward to hearing from any one who 'talks' Penobscot Bay Light Houses.
Ernest & Pauline (Fitzgerald) DeRAPS
RR #1, Box 1213
Hallowell, Maine 04347

Enclosed:
Resume of Service & Poem
The Lighthouse Keeper's Lament

Resume of Service
Ernest G. DeRAPS,
U.S. Coast Guard — Retired

Oct. 1955 - Aug.1956 10 months	Rockland Base, Rockland, Maine Leading Seaman - Asst. Cook
Aug. '56 - Dec. '57 16 months	Monhegan Island L/S (Rockland Group) Single Family Light House (Primary [First Order] Light) Officer -in-Charge

Dec. '57 - Oct. '59
22 months
	Fort Point L/S, Stockton Springs, Maine (Rockland Group)
	Single Family Light House (Secondary [Fourth Order] Light)
	  Fog Signal Bell
	  Officer-in-Charge

Oct. '59 - Jul. '61
21 months
	Heron Neck L/S, Greens Island, Maine (Rockland Group)
	Three man (Stag) Station, semi-isolated (Secondary Light)
	  Siren Fog Signal
	  Engineering Officer - Standby O.-in-C.

Jul. '61 - Nov. '62 16 months	Brown's Head L/S, Vinalhaven Island, ME. (Rockland Grp.) Single Family Light House (Secondary [Fourth Order] Light) Officer -in-Charge
Nov. '62 - Oct. '64 23 months	USCG Cutter COOS BAY (WAVP-376) Maine State Pier; Portland, Maine
Oct. '64 - Sept. '65 11 months	USCG Cutter BARATARIA (WAVP-381) Maine State Pier; Portland, Maine
Sep. '65 - Mar. '68 29.5 months	USCG Base; So. Portland, Maine Worked with "Captain -of-the-Port" OOD; JOOD; Designated "Dangerous Cargoman"
Mar. '68 - Aug. '68 5 months	USCG Cutter CASTLE ROCK (WHEC-383) Maine State Pier; Portland, Maine
Aug. '68 - Jan. '69	USCG First Dist. Hdqts. and USPub. Health Serv. Hospital
July 1974	Permanent Disability. Retirement!

4/19/94

Dear Mr. & Mrs. DeRaps:

I just received this month's issue of Lighthouse Digest, *and I enjoyed reading your letter.*

When I was in Maine visiting my family, I met a teacher with a passion for lighthouses. Since then, I have made lighthouses my hobby. It has only been about 5 years, so I am not as extremely informed as others, but I am eagerly seeking to add to my understanding and knowledge of lighthouses. Since information is so scarce, I am anxious to witness the production of your book! Lighthouse keepers like you have so many great experiences to share. Soon this world will not have the privilege of hearing actual lighthouse stories from the keepers themselves.

The only lighthouses I have been to are those in the Bath area of Maine. The two Penobscot Bay lights I have seen are Owls Head and Pemaquid. Oh! Also the Rockland Breakwater Light. In the future I hope to visit many more, including ones closer to home in Washington State.

Well, it is more than an honor to me to think that these words will be read by an actual lighthouse keeper! I'm glad you gave your address.

I have just received my elementary teaching certificate and am in a temporary position as a 5th grade teacher. Of course, all my students have heard many tidbits of lighthouse lore and history. They will be excited to learn that I wrote to you, and we would be greatly honored to receive a reply - even just an autograph. (Do you feel like a movie star yet?)

Thank you for taking the time out of your busy schedule to read this letter. Best wishes to you, your Family and your book. God bless your hard work!

Sincerely,
Ruth Bearscove

Sunday 15 May, 1994

Dear Ms. Bearscove and 5th Graders,

I was greatly surprised and pleased to receive your letter of April 19. I am happy that you enjoyed my letter to the editor. Yours is the only response thus far from readers of the Lighthouse Digest, *perhaps there are few former keepers who know of, or subscribe to, the* Digest.

The lighthouses you mention as having visited, in your letter, are quite familiar to me. While stationed at the Coast Guard Base; Rockland, Maine, in the early part of my Coast Guard tenure, I was made aware of the Penobscot Bay ones as they were visible from the Base. The Rockland Breakwater Lighthouse is most prominent as it protects the entrance to Rockland Harbor and was on the extreme end of a one mile long breakwater built of granite blocks. Owls Head Lighthouse is on the Mainland just south and a little east of the harbor entrance. The Pemaquid Lighthouse and those Lighthouses in the Bath area did not come under the jurisdiction of the Rockland Base, therefore I knew little of them at that time. Pauline and I, with family members, have since visited the very picturesque Pemaquid Lighthouse. It now serves as a small coastal museum. Another very interesting place to visit, is the Lighthouse Museum

now operating in Rockland, Maine.

Lighthouses and memorabilia from them should be a very interesting hobby. My wife and I have a small collection of such materials and quite a few books related to Lighthouses and their keepers. Things we have collected and kept over the years. Among some of my more prized Lighthouse memorabilia, are the many colored slides taken while stationed at the various Lighthouses where we served as Keepers. Pauline, my wife, and I have been honored to make several slide presentations shown to local groups and to some local school classes. From these slides I will have photographs printed which will make up the major portion of my book, which I intend to publish as a photo-journal. I have already typed an outline for the book and brief introductions to 5 of the 7 intended chapters. The book is temporarily on hold, for the summer, as I am doing some part-time carpentry for one of my daughters and her husband.

I have enclosed a copy of my resume of Service which your 5th grade class might find of interest. You might note that the first C.G. Cutter on which I served was named "Coos Bay" after a Bay and Community in your neighboring State of Oregon. If your class has one or two questions regarding Lighthouse Keeping, please forward them and I will attempt to answer them in a future letter. Perhaps with the publishers and their permission, I might be able to include them in my book.

I wish to thank you for responding to my "Lighthouse Digest" letter.

Sincerely
Ernest G. DeRAPS
U.S. Coast Guard, Retired

May 23, 1994

Dear Mr. DeRaps

Thank you for answering our letter and sending us the book and other information. It would be fun to have our questions in your book. Here are some of the questions we would like to ask you.

1. *What are your daily duties?*
2. *Is it hard to keep a lighthouse?*
3. *What are lighthouses made of?*
4. *How tall are lighthouses?*
5. *Did you enjoy being a lighthouse keeper?*
6. *Did you get homesick?*
7. *Did any of your children live at the lighthouse?*
8. *Did your children go to school?*
9. *Did you have any problems getting the lighthouse to work?*

Thank you again for your time, and we look forward to hearing from you.

Sincerely,

Ruth Bearscove & Class

Ques. 1. What are your daily duties?

The first and foremost duty of a Light House Keeper is to maintain his navigational aid, the LIGHT and if one is on station, the FOG SIGNAL. Maintenance consists of cleaning all mechanisms to keep them operating properly. If it is a rotating lens the clock works weights must be wound up as need and the rotation must be properly timed to accurately create the designated light flashes and dark intervals between flashes to allow positive identification of the signal by a mariner. The lens and tower lantern must be kept as clean and dust free as possible to allow maximum visibility. A keeper must be punctual in lighting the light at 1/2 hour before sunset and keeping it lighted until 1/2 hour after sunrise. All lenses should be covered during daylight hours when not in operation as the bright sun and its heat is bad for them. Some lighthouses are also lighted during fog, rain, snow and any cause of poor visibility. Fog signals must be properly timed to give their designated signals at the proper interval designated by the Coast Guards' book "Local List of Lights and other Marine Aids." A ship's location can be determined by sightings of Lighthouses, other Aids to Navigation and then consulting the above mentioned book.

A second duty is to maintain the buildings of an assigned station, accomplishing minor repairs and painting all structures as needed. Buildings at a station may consist of dwellings for one or more keepers, generator buildings, garages, coal bins, paint lockers and fog bell towers.

A Station Log (record book) must be kept of weather conditions at 8 A.M., Noon, 4 and 8 P.M. and any unusual happenings that occur. Maintenance of vehicles, generators and other machinery must also be recorded. Old Glory should be raised at 8 A.M. each morning and lowered at sunset. There is also a continual receipt of mail with orders to do this or that or forms requesting information and sometimes, reminders to complete certain maintenance or repairs.

Ques. 2. Is it hard to keep a lighthouse?

Not unlike other jobs where a person is somewhat on his own, if a keeper plans ahead, schedules his work, uses his time wisely and keeps busy; the job isn't too difficult. It is when there are outside interruptions that the job can become hectic and sometimes worrisome. Unexpected demands on a keeper's routine work and his time can cause some problems.

Of course various stations demand different things. At Monhegan Island Light Station the only navigational aid was the light; a first order lens (about six feet in diameter and eight feet tall). It took a lot of time to polish, dust and clean such a lens, especially with the IOV (Incandescent Oil Vapor) lamp as a light source. The lantern surrounding the lens was about 12 feet in diameter and I guess about 9 feet tall with 10 or 12 one inch thick plate glass panes.

A fourth order lens, like the one at Fort Point Light Station, was very much smaller than a first order lens. The fourth order lens was usually only a foot to eighteen inches in diameter and from two to three feet tall and it stood on a pedestal. And of course the glass lantern was proportionally smaller and had steel plates at the bottom with the glass panes at the top. This light used an electric light bulb as a light source, and commercial electricity with a generator as stand-by power.

At Fort Point L/S the keeper was also responsible for maintaining a second navigational aid, a Fog Bell which needed much attention. The Fog Signal, striking of the 1/2 ton Paul Revere bell, was done by a large cast iron hammer like device which was timed and actuated by a brass clock mechanism. The clock was run by gravity - similar to a coo-coo clock. For gravity to do the work, first the keeper had to work. He had to wind a ton of weight up a shaft manually, then as gravity pulled

the weight down, the brass clockworks slowed the descent of the weight and timed the striking of the bell. One strike every 20 seconds which equals three times each minute.

At Heron Neck L/S, both the light source in the tower and the fog signal siren were operated electrically even though there was no commercial electric power. As the station engineer, it was my responsibility to maintain the two gasoline powered electric generators.

At Brown's Head L/S there were two Navigational Aids also, the light (with 1 white and 2 red sectors) and a Fog Signal bell. Both were operated by commercial electric power generated in the town of Vinalhaven and the station had a stand-by generator for power outages. The bell at this station was struck electrically through the use of a timed electric solenoid.

For some lighthouse keepers, the hardest part of their job was the paperwork. They had to write their reports, maintain their many log books and keep their records.

Ques. 3. What are lighthouses made of?

Many light house towers were constructed of granite which was quarried here in the State of Maine. Some at Vinalhaven Island, Hurricane Island which is South West of Vinalhaven and some quarried even in Hallowell, Maine, where Polly and I have lived for the past 25 years.

Other light towers were constructed of bricks & mortar, stones & cement and some, like Goose Rocks L/S, were even constructed of steel plates.

Some of the keepers' dwellings were also constructed of granite blocks, especially those at very exposed areas where the ocean could reach them during storms. The majority of dwellings, however, were constructed of lumber which is much lighter, easier to work with and much easier to transport, especially by boat.

Monhegan Island's light tower was conical and constructed of large granite blocks about 2 feet thick, 3 feet tall and about 5 feet long at the base. The blocks became progressively shorter as the tower diameter lessened near the top. The lantern structure, the platform beneath it and the platforms safety railings were made of steel, as they are at most light towers.

The light towers at Fort Point L/S, Heron Neck L/S and Browns Head L/S were all constructed of bricks and mortar. Fort Points light tower was square and vertical or plumb, on the outside but was round inside. Heron Neck and Browns Head light towers were conical and were round inside as well as out.

A few light towers, located in Southern Florida among the keys and reefs, are skeleton like structures of iron or steel beams. They were constructed to withstand hurricane force winds and heavy seas.

At Cape Henry, Virginia, where the first lighthouse built by the Federal Government once stood, there was and perhaps still is, a light tower constructed of cast iron plates. This tower was originally built in 1791.

Portland Head Lighthouse at Cape Elizabeth, Maine, was originally commissioned by the Massachusetts Colony in 1790 and construction was started. This was 30 years before Maine became a State of the Union. The original station was completed in 1791.

Ques. 4. How tall are lighthouses?

Lighthouse towers vary in height according to their location and local navigational needs. Coastal lighthouses tend to be of much higher elevation above the ocean waters than those lighthouses in more protected bays and rivers.

At Monhegan Island which is 10 miles from the mainland in the Atlantic Ocean, the tower is about forty feet tall, but it was located on the highest part of the island and 178 feet above the ocean's waters. Because of its height and candlepower, this light could be seen for 20 miles.

Fort Point Lighthouse tower is only about fifteen feet tall but stands on a cliff above the upper Penobscot Bay at 88 feet above the water. It is visible in clear weather for about 15 miles.

Rockland Breakwater Lighthouse tower is only thirty-nine feet above the Bay and harbor waters, built on a granite pier and can be seen for 11 miles in clear weather.

The tallest tower structure that I am aware of is the Fire Island Lighthouse which rises 167 feet above the low South Shore of Long Island (N.Y.). It is one of the most important navigational aids to ships bound for New York City's harbor.

Ques. 5. Did you enjoy being a lighthouse keeper?

Yes, and for several reasons. As Officer-in-Charge and Keeper of a Family Lighthouse (Monhegan, Fort Point and Browns Head), I lived with my wife and children. I have always been very "Family" oriented and enjoyed having my family near me, watching the children grow and helping to teach them in the many aspects of life.

I have always enjoyed meeting people and making new friends. Lighthouses attract many visitors and it was always a pleasure for my wife Polly and I to greet these guests and make them welcome. We were an Official Arm of the United States Coast Guard and servants of the public. As long as our hospitality didn't interfere with our station duties, we were happy to "show case" our duty stations!

Pauline was, and still is, a conscientious and clean housekeeper, so our stations were always ready for guests or inspection.

I also enjoyed the fact that as Officer-in-Charge, I was somewhat my own boss. I certainly had some specific duties, some of which were on a strict schedule. But the fact that my Commanding Officers put their trust in me to meet the challenges set before me and to get the job done without constant supervision has always been an uplifting factor in my Lighthouse career.

Ques. 6. Did you get homesick?

An old saying states, "Home is where a man's HAT is!" I prefer another saying, "Home is where a man's HEART is!"

Since our marriage, home and my heart have always been where Pauline my wife is, and of course as the children arrived they were included in that home! When living together on a Family Light Station, the lighthouse became our home.

However, when I was stationed at Heron Neck L/S, (the men only station), I certainly missed my family and that can definitely be termed "Homesick!" I remedied that situation as quickly as I could and brought my family to Vinalhaven Island, about as near to me as they could be.

We really became a family again when stationed at Brown's Head L/S. However, that was somewhat short lived.

After serving at the lighthouses, I was transferred to "Sea Duty." Then I was truly homesick, especially when at sea on the 30 plus days at sea on weather patrol. Several times I was away from home for three months. Not only did I become homesick, I also was occasionally "seasick." That, however, is another story and perhaps another book!

Ques. 7 Did any of your children live at the lighthouse?

When we arrived for duty at our first Family Lighthouse, Monhegan Island L/S, our first child Thomas was just 21 months old. While assigned to this same L/S, in late January of 1957, our second child arrived. Lisa was born at the hospital in Belfast, Maine—off island. But, at the age of 2 or so weeks in mid-February she and her Mom, Polly, boated out to Monhegan Island and back to the L/S.

Both Thomas and Lisa also lived at Fort Point L/S in Stockton Springs, Maine, as well as Brown's Head L/S on Vinalhaven Island.

Our two middle children, Patricia (Patti) and Peter lived with us at Browns Head L/S. Peter was born during our tenure at this Light Station.

Denise and Scott came to complete our family of six children, after I had been assigned aboard various Coast Guard Weather Cutter vessels. They, therefore, have never been fortunate enough to live at a lighthouse.

Ques. 8. Did your children go to school?

Most certainly. They all received their high school diplomas. Thomas worked his way through college (five years) and is an ordained minister. Lisa obtained further education by joining the U. S. Navy. Patricia obtained local training and worked for many years at the Bath Ironworks, a shipyard making vessels for the Navy. Peter, at this writing, has completed over 16 years of service in a career as a U.S. Marine. Denise, after a short time at college, was told by her guidance counselor that she had sufficient knowledge and training to fulfill her desire to become a secretary. She obtained a job and left the university. Scott did a stint in the U. S. Air Force but didn't care for it.

Of course, I assume the question about schooling refers to the time of our lighthouse duties. To answer that question, "Yes!". When I was stationed at Heron Neck L/S, Thomas started school as a kindergartner at the Vinalhaven Elementary School. While at Brown's Head L/S, he attended the First Grade, also at Vinalhaven.

Ques. 9. Did you have any problems getting the lighthouse to work?

The most difficult light to operate was the Incandescent Oil Vapor lamp (IOV) at Monhegan Island L/S. The kerosene oil had to be absolutely free of any minute particles which could clog up the .001 inch nozzle orifice or filter. The vaporizer tube had to be heated by an alcohol torch every time one lighted the mantle which was the light source. In very cold winter weather, it was sometimes difficult to heat the vaporizer tube sufficiently for the kerosene oil to become a vapor. At other times, even though the light might have been lighted and burning for several hours, if the temperature inside the lantern became sufficiently cold, the light could become less bright and dimmed due to poor vaporization. Another difficulty at Monhegan Island L/S was the maintenance and timing of the brass & steel clock works mechanism and weight system used to rotate the large and heavy lens. The clock works had to occasionally be adjusted to make sure the lens made one complete revolution every eight minutes. This rotation created the prescribed 5.6 second flash of light every 60 seconds (each minute).

I believe the next most difficult operation was not a light but the Fog Signal (Bell) at Fort Point L/S. The clock works mechanism was very old and hard to adjust for the proper timing of the bell signal. The tower weights which were used to run the clock had to be wound up frequently when the fog signal was in operation. This combination of the gravitational force of the dropping weights and the clock works mechanism were used to actuate the hammer which struck the bell. When operating during poor visibility, the prescribed signal interval was 1 stroke every 20 seconds (3 strikes per minute).

I apologize for the lateness of the foregoing answers to your questions, but hope I have included sufficient information. Memories are wonderful, the pleasant and some not so. But as one ages it seems that their head holds so many good and bad memories it is sometimes hard to sort them out. Writing some of them, as I have done in this book, often brings to mind other memories long ago forgotten. As our lighthouse tenure was some 35 to 40 years prior to the writing of this journal - 1956 to 1962 - I'm sure there must be some errors. Please forgive my faulty memory!

10 June, 1994

Pauline & Ernest

My wife and myself are "NEW" readers of the Lighthouse Digest, *but not new to the duties of Lighthouse Keeping.*

We started back in 1946, when I got stationed on Baker's Island Light, Salem Harbor, Mass. I was asst. keeper on that light for 5 years. We went out to that island with 2 sons and came off with 3 sons and a daughter. That was in 1951.

In 1952, I was stationed on good old Monhegan and added another daughter to our Coast Guard Family. We left Monhegan, October 1954 (because of the school system there) and Henley Day took over, when we left.

In the summer of '52, I got tired of the oil lamps we were using to light the rooms in the house, so I wired the down stairs rooms. It drove the islanders nuts, trying to figure out how the lights were so bright. That summer, we brought the first TV to the island and again the islanders went nuts - they all wanted to know, "What's that thing on the lighthouse roof?"! It was the TV antenna.

Was the "I.O.V." system still being used in the light when you were there? Have you two been back to the Island? My wife and I went back for a day visit a couple of years ago and were surprised to see the house is now a museum. We have a lot of stories of the Light House days, but putting them down on paper — no way!

So some day if we're up there or you come down here, maybe we'll talk.

Till then,
Paul & Helen Baptiste

July 13, 1994

Dear Ernest and Pauline,

I got your name from the Lighthouse Digest *and found it interesting that you are working on a book concerning your past duties as a Lighthouse Keeper.*

I'm sorry to say I'm not a former Keeper (however, I am a "Keeper Member" of the Lighthouse Preservation Society). For quite some time I have been a great Lighthouse buff and, in fact, my husband and I came close to purchasing a Lighthouse along the Oregon coast.

I, too, am currently at work on a novel which is set in Maine and the central focus being a lighthouse. I have been a professional freelance writer for over sixteen years and an active member of The Author's Guild of America for ten years. My work has appeared in several major newspapers and magazines throughout the U.S.

I have only been to Maine once (in Millinocket), and fell in love instantly with the people and scenery.

I feel individuals such as yourselves would be a most interesting topic for an article I'm researching for Atlantic Monthly magazine and would like to know if I could further correspond in asking you questions about your past duties as Keeper of three Maine Light Stations.

If I can be of any help to you with your book, please don't hesitate to let me know.

I'll look forward to hearing from you at your earliest convenience.

Sincerely,
JoMarie Grinkiewicz

18 October 1994

Dear JoMarie,

Please forgive my long delay in answering your letter of July 13th. I am recuperating from a hospital stay at our local Veterans' Administration Hospital and a two week vacation trip with my wife Pauline (Polly), two of our daughters and our "nearly five" year old grandson. Our trip took us over 3,500 miles in 9 days of driving during our 12 days away from Maine. The girls did a good deal of the driving. We had a great visit with our son (a U.S. Marine with 15 years service), his wife and their two year old daughter in Havelock, NC. We also visited; a nephew in Connecticut, a nephew and two niece and their families in New Jersey, my sister-in-law and one of her daughters families in South Carolina, the mother-in-law of our daughter Patricia, living at Amelia Island, Florida - just north of Jacksonville, an old friend whom we hadn't seen in nearly 30 years who lives in Valdosta, Georgia and lastly, we visited the beautiful Luray Caverns in Virginia's Appalachian Mountains near the Shenandoah National Park and Skyline Drive.

My "Book Writing" has been on hold during our very busy summer, but I intend to get back to work on it this month.

Although I am retired, I am actively involved in several local organizations and quite frequently drive Senior Citizens on day trips in our van. I also am Publisher/Editor of our Family Newsletter which has been published quarterly since July 1981. Just prior to departing on our 12 day vacation trip, I mailed issue #54 which was of average length - 29 - 8 1/2 X 11 inch - pages plus a two sided cover sheet.

The Newsletter was delivered to 43 current subscribers from Maine to California and into Canada who each pay $12.50 per year to cover the cost of duplication (copying) and mailing. This Family Newsletter helps to keep our large family close in spirit and informed of FAMILY happenings. As the youngest sibling of our parents 14 children, I have the pleasure of being the "Family Historian" and "Genealogist!" Needless to say, the record keeping and computer keyboarding for these two projects can be quite time consuming.

In regard to your request to further correspond, asking questions, etc., about my past Light House Keeping duties; I will be happy to respond, provided that I may use such information given to you in my own writings and book.

I am also corresponding with a teacher and her 5th grade class in Auburn, Washington. The class have asked several questions which I shall answer in future letters and I intend to include this information in my upcoming book.

Thank you for responding to my Lighthouse Digest *letter. I was pleased to receive your letter and included a copy of it in our #54 Family Newsletter of October 1994. I look forward to hearing from you again soon and promise to be more prompt in answering.*

Sincerely,
Ernest G. DeRAPS
U.S.C.G. Retired

Daniel B. Niven
Astoria, Oregon
June 1, 1994
Dear Mr. DeRaps,

I was just catching up on some back issues of Lighthouse Digest, and I saw your letter on page 25 of the April 1994 issue, just above the short article on "MY" lighthouse, C.G. Light Station New Dungeness. My wife Emily and I were the keepers at New Dungeness Light (NDL) from April 1992 to June 1993. Of course NDL is boarded up now, but we were lucky enough to spend our entire year-plus tour out there during which talk of closure was still in the background. NDL, as some people are aware (more, now that she's closed) was the other lighthouse the Coast Guard maintained full-time with its own people. Now, of course, Boston Light is the only one remaining.

A few items about our lives as keepers. The assignment opened up every spring to an E-3, married, with no kids. About 10 or 12 couples applied for it every year. The most exciting element of our job was the 5-mile beach transit along the spit to and from the light; we had to do it on a low tide, and from time to time our chain saw and/or winch on the 4wheel drive were a necessity in getting from point A to point B. Due to the lack of low enough tides during part of the winter, our 11-foot inflatable boat was our means of transport to and from the mainland. The light was automated in 1976, so our primary duties were to give tours to visitors (60+, on a good day) who had walked, ridden horses, or kayaked over, and maintain the grounds and buildings. We also called in WX obs. (weather observations) every 3 hours, and assisted in a couple of SARs (Search and Rescue efforts).

People often asked my wife if she was in the Coast Guard as well, and she would reply, "No, but this is probably the closest I'll come!" When she wasn't assisting me with tours, she could often be found with paintbrush in hand. Since Saturdays and Sundays were our busiest days, our "weekend" was Tuesday and Wednesday, when we closed up shop and could leave the light. (Posted signs listed tour hours 9 - 4, Thursday to Monday.)

I'm now a QM3 on the Coast Guard Cutter RESOLUTE (WMEC-620), but keep involved with lighthouse lore and maritime history. I'm a docent at the Columbia River Maritime Museum here in town and just yesterday gave a lighthouse talk to a couple of 2nd grade reading classes who had just finished Keep the Lights Burning, Abbie.

If you'd like some more information on lighthouses on the west coast, or — my specialty — in the Pacific Northwest, I can probably help. Also, we have an MK1 on the boat who was once stationed at Isles of Shoals Light (in the Atlantic, near the Maine/New Hampshire border) for a while, if firsthand info from him would be helpful. Drop me a line if you have any questions, or just to "talk" lighthouses, as you say!

Sincerely,
Dan Niven

Now that you have finished reading my side of this journal, please close this book, rotate it 180 degrees and read what my good wife has written as **HER** *side of the story.*